HANDBOOK TO HALL MARKS

ON

GOLD AND SILVER PLATE

HANDBOOK TO HALL MARKS

ON

GOLD & SILVER PLATE

OF

GREAT BRITAIN AND IRELAND

by

WILLIAM CHAFFERS

WITH TABLES OF THE ANNUAL DATE LETTERS
EMPLOYED IN THE ASSAY OFFICES

TEXT AND DATE TABLES EXTENDED, CORRECTED
AND REVISED

BY

CYRIL G. E. BUNT

Of the Victoria and Albert Museum

LONDON
WILLIAM REEVES

736
Chaffers

Published by
WILLIAM REEVES Bookseller Ltd
1a Norbury Crescent, London, S.W.16

© 1969 William Reeves Bookseller Ltd

First Edition published 1897
Tenth Edition, Revised, 1969

Made in England

Printed in Great Britain by
Lowe & Brydone (Printers) Ltd., London

PREFACE

It is hoped that this work will be useful to all those who require, in a convenient form, information respecting the marks on gold and silver, for the purpose of readily fixing the date and office of assay of any piece of plate. The continued popularity of this handbook, which was first published in 1897, proves the unquestioned need for such a convenient reference book.

In this edition, the Irish section has been re-written, the latest date letters of all offices have been added and certain inaccuracies corrected.

A word may perhaps here be said about the marks. It should be understood that they give as close an approximation as possible to the appearance of the original stamps. The claim made in some books that drawings of marks are facsimilies is of course absurd. For all practical purposes it will be found that the marks given in the following pages are sufficiently close for identification. Bearing in mind that the punch marks are too often carelessly struck and have frequently been rendered still less clear by years of too industrious cleaning, one is not infrequently led to identification as much by knowing what a mark is likely to be, as by its actual appearance.

Our thanks are due to the assay masters, who have so kindly furnished information, to enable us to complete the various alphabets.

Many of the letters included in the tables of London Assay Office letters were the copyright of the late Mr. W. J. Cripps, c.b., f.s.a., author of "Old English Plate" and by the courtesy and express permission of his representatives they are used in this book.

The publishers are indebted to Capt. Ronald Le Bas of the Assay Office, Dublin, for his kindly help and advice.

The publishers would welcome any suggestions for improvements or information which may be of assistance for future editions of this handbook.

CONTENTS

HOW TO READ "HALL MARKS"

To every gold and silversmith, to every assistant in "the trade," to every antique dealer, the ability to read the marks on plate is of great importance. To an equal extent, it may be said, must it be of interest to the amateur—almost, one might assume, to the man in the street—to be able to identify these marks exactly. For they will enable him to discover the quality, the date and place of origin—in many cases even the name of the maker—of any piece of plate or object in the precious metals he may possess.

This, it will readily be understood, is the whole *raison d'être* of this little handbook; and these few words are only intended to make as easy as possible what is, after all, not quite an easy task even for the specialist.

If the aspirant to efficiency has already glanced through these pages he will have realised that, important as the series of four or five individual stamps may be as a whole, he must yet consider each separately if he is to arrive at exact knowledge of their purport.

Suppose for a moment we are quite unlearned in the matter and wish to determine all we can about a piece we have acquired. We look carefully at it and find it has four stamps as follows : —

We see first of all the leopard's head. It is crowned and is enclosed in a sunken outline following the shape of the head. We may call this a "shaped outline" to distinguish it from a definite shield. This of course is the town mark—the mark of the London Hall of Assay, Goldsmith's Hall— and reference to the appropriate pages of this book will show that in this form it was in use before 1673. Passing next to the lion passant, which denotes the standard quality of the gold or silver, we see that this, too, is in a shaped outline.

Enquiry into the changing form of this standard mark shows that it was used thus from 1558 to 1678. Taking these two marks together we know that our piece of plate must have been stamped in London between 1558 and 1673.

We can now look at our third mark—the date letter L. A glance at the date lists will show that the only cycle of black letter capitals extends from 1658-1678. The letter in question indicates that it was assayed in 1668-69.

Finally we have the maker's mark, J.R., which we may or may not be able to identify—our handbook does not lay itself out to give lists of these—but this is usually less important than the particulars we have described.

It should be especially noted that the shape of the shield, coupled with the device, is always of greatest importance. Especially is this the case with the date letter, since in certain cycles similar alphabets occur which may otherwise be confused. So important is this question of the shape of the shield that too great attention cannot be directed to it.

THE PROCESS OF ASSAYING

IT will be understood from what has already been said that the presence of hall marks upon any piece of plate is in the nature of a guarantee (a) of the place of assay, (b) the year in which the assay was carried out, and (c) the standard of quality of the precious metals.

Obviously the last is the most important consideration and, indeed, the other two marks would not be impressed if, by intention or accident, the quality were not up to standard.

The test is carried out under the strictest conditions by "good men and true" acting as representatives of the Goldsmiths' Company.

The method of test in vogue in earlier times—still practised often enough as a rough test—was by means of the touchstone (*pierre de touche*). The touchstone was a slab of black siliceous slate, upon which a "streak" was made with the gold or silver to be tested. The assayer then proceeded to test this streak, by comparison with similar streaks made with his touch needles. One set of these was alloyed with copper and another with silver (for touch of gold); and a set for silver was alloyed with lead.

It has been said that the difference of half a karat can be distinguished in this way; but it must be admitted that at best it is a rough and ready mode which cannot compare with the method of assay by cupellation.

This method depends upon the removal by chemical action of all the alloy of base metal and a comparison by weight with a like quantity of pure metal. It is a method of great antiquity—the "refiner's fire" of the Bible—and well known in Roman times.

The process for gold may be briefly described thus: a scraping weighing some eight or ten grains is taken from the object to be assayed, and after being carefully weighed, it is added to two and a half times its weight of silver. These are then wrapped in a piece of thin sheet lead—again of proportionate weight, and the tiny parcel is placed in a small crucible called a *cupel*, made of bone ashes. When heated in the muffle stove the metals melt and the gold and silver combine, but the lead, plus the base metal of the alloy, oxidise and are absorbed by the cupel.

The gold and silver pellet is then flattened out and made into a "cornet" and, being placed in hot nitric acid, the silver dissolves and the gold is left. The pure gold is then weighed and the difference between the weight of the original scrapings and the residue give the quantity of alloy.

The process for silver is much the same. The scraping is wrapped in its cover of sheet lead and the pellet placed in the cupel and fired. Again oxidisation takes place and the residue of pure silver is left.

A scraping is actually taken from each separate part of any object being assayed and the minute portion of metal so taken for examination is carefully preserved. It is called "the diet."

ARTICLES EXEMPT FROM ASSAY

ALTHOUGH it is compulsory for all domestic gold and silver plate, watch-cases and wedding rings to be hall marked after assay, there are certain objects which are (or perhaps we should say may be), exempt, either because of their small size or because to impress the hall mark upon them would deface their ornamentation.

Reference to the chronological table will show that, by the Act of 1738, certain wares in gold and silver were exempt from the obligation of assay. Such wares, made in great numbers and enormous variety included every conceivable type of knick-knack of use or ornament, and for their manufacture Birmingham and Sheffield were renowned.

These small articles were produced largely by skilled specialists in such "lines," who were known in Birmingham as "toymen," and their wares were famous all over the civilised world. Trinkets of gold and silver, ivory, tortoiseshell, enamels and so forth, besides jewellery proper, sword-hilts, gun and dagger ornaments, buttons, buckles, snuff-box mounts were included. A visitor to Milan towards the end of the seventeenth century, speaking of the " fine works of rock-crystal, swords, heads of canes, snuff-boxes and other fine works," observed "They can be had cheaper and better at Birmingham."

The articles exempt from assay by the Act of 1738 and which the toyman and others were permitted to make and sell without licence may be listed as follows : —

Jewellers' work, set with jewels or stones; jointed night ear-rings of gold; finger rings (except wedding rings and mourning rings); chains, necklaces and necklace beads; watch and seal chains; lockets; buttons (hollow or raised); thimbles; cranes for bottles; coral sockets and bells; ferrules, pipe-lighters, small book-clasps; jointed stock and garter clasps; snuff and patch-box rims (when the box is of tortoiseshell or carved stone); gun, pistol, sword and dagger mounts; toothpick, tweezer, pencil and needle cases; filigree work; the mounts, screws or stoppers of glass bottles.

While the list just given has still statutory effect as regards gold, a later act (30 Geo. III) in 1790 repealed these exemptions in respect of silver and brought others into force. These included : silver jewellery in which precious or other stones are set (excepting mourning rings); silver chains, beads for necklaces, lockets, filigree, shirt buckles or brooches, stamped medals, spouts to teapots (of china, etc.). These were total exemptions. In addition, silver tippings, swages and mounts of less than 10 dwts.

(except necks or collars for castors, cruets, etc.) and certain silver articles weighing less than 5 dwts. were exempt. There were many exceptions to the latter, however, such as : necks, collars or tops for castors, etc.; buttons, wrought or blank seals, bottle labels, shoe clasps, patch boxes, salt spoons, tea spoons and strainers, caddy spoons, buckles (other than those mentioned earlier) and pieces to garnish cabinets, boxes, etc.

Although these and many other small articles were exempt from *compulsory* assay, they were frequently submitted for test and were then, of course, stamped in the ordinary way. That is why in lists of charges such as those given in a return made to the Board of Trade, by order of the House of Commons in December, 1893, most of those articles are included.

The charges made have increased since then and are liable to fluctuation, being regulated by the Goldsmiths' Companies. No useful purpose would be served in quoting recent charges since at any time, in consequence of economic conditions, they can be altered.

It is definitely laid down that if the amount received for assay should exceed expenses, the balance should be utilised to help pay for prosecutions for fraud, or alternatively the charges might be reduced. So far as London is concerned the expenses invariably exceed the receipts.

2

CHRONOLOGICAL TABLE

1238.   The Mayor and Aldermen of London to select six good men and true to see that no gold or silver articles were made of metal inferior to that of the coinage.

1300.   The Goldsmiths' Company put on a sound basis. The leopard's head, "Une teste de leopart," selected as the standard mark. (28 Ed. I).

1327.   (Ed. III). The Goldsmiths' Company incorporated by charter.

1336.   An ordinance of the Goldsmiths' Company decreed the use of the leopard's head crowned, the assay and maker's marks on all plate.

1355.   The trial plate introduced at the assay office.

1378.   (2 Rich. II). Every goldsmith to have his own proper mark upon his work, together with the mark of the city or borough and the assayer's mark "appointed by the king."

1401. The gold standard reduced to 16 karats.

1423. (2 Hen. VI). The touch of the leopard's head and mark or touch of the workman. Seven assay towns were appointed by this act—York, Newcastle, Norwich, Lincoln, Bristol, Coventry and Salisbury.

1477. (17 Ed. IV). The leopard's head crowned and the mark of the worker. The standard of 18 karats (gold) restored. (No gold under 18 karats fine allowed to be worked or sold, nor any silver under sterling.)

1512. (Reign of Henry VIII). Enormous destruction of ecclesiastical plate.

1513. (5 Hen. VIII). Again it is ordained that the maker must put his mark on his work and also the assayer the date letter and that the wardens shall mark it with the leopard's head crowned.

1519. The leopard's head changes form. It is still crowned, but within a shaped outline.

1544. The standard mark the lion passant, guardant, crowned within a shaped outline.

1548. The standard mark changed to the lion passant, guardant, uncrowned in rectangular shape.

1558. The standard mark as above but in a shaped outline—continued until 1678.

1560. Since this date the date letter has been enclosed in a shield varying in form.

1576. (18 Eliz.). "No goldsmith should work, sell or exchange any wares of gold less in fineness than 22 karats . . . nor . . . of silver less in fineness than 11 ozs. 2 dwts. . . . nor put on sale any wares before he has set his own mark on so much thereof as might conveniently bear the same.''

1597.   The minutes of the Goldsmiths' Company refer to the standard mark as '' Her Majesty's lion '' (the first mention of the lion passant). The alphabetical date letter was approved and the use of the leopard's head was limited by statute.

1675.   An order re-enforced the standard of 22 karat gold and sterling silver—to be marked with the lion and leopard's head crowned or one of them. A touch plate to be kept at Goldsmiths' Hall.

1678.   The leopard's head again in circle. The shape enclosing the lion again changed.

1697-8. (8 and 9 Will. III). The new, Britannia, standard of silver introduced. The figure of Britannia and the lion's head erased. The maker's mark the two first letters of his surname.

1700-1. (12 and 13 Will. III). The towns of York, Exeter, Bristol, Chester and Norwich re-appointed to assay plate. They were to stamp it with the marks of the lion's head erased and Britannia, the assay mark of their town and variable date letter in roman characters.

1701.   (1 Anne). Newcastle added to the foregoing as an assay town.

1719.   (6 Geo. I). The old standard of silver restored; also the old assay marks—the lion, leopard's head, maker's mark and date letter. But both standards were allowed simultaneously, the appropriate marks being employed. The lion in a rectangle.

1738.   (12 Geo. II). The maker's mark changed to "the initials of christian and surname." The shield of the leopard's head altered to one similar to that of date letter.

Certain wares in gold and silver exempt from assay.

1773.   (13 Geo. III). The lion in a shaped outline. Birmingham and Sheffield were appointed assay towns for silver plate.

1784.   (24 Geo. III). Duty mark of the king's head to be stamped on articles. The lion in an ellipse, but this was soon changed to a regular shield.

1785.   (25 Geo. III). Drawback stamp of Britannia discontinued.

1798.   (38 Geo. III). The standard of 18 karat gold reintroduced—to be marked with a crown and the figures 18.

1828.   (5 Geo. IV). Birmingham empowered to assay and stamp gold.

1844.   (7 and 8 Vict.). Gold of 22 karats to be stamped with a crown and "22," instead of the lion passant.

1854.   (17 and 18 Vict.). Reduced standards of gold allowed to be stamped—15, 12 and 9 karats—without the crown and king's head.

1867.   Foreign plate, when assayed, to be marked with "F" in addition to the usual marks of the hall.

1890.   (54 Vict.). The duty of 17s. per oz. on gold and 1s. 6d. per oz. on silver plate abolished. The sovereign's head duty mark discontinued.

1904.   (4 Ed. VII). Foreign plate to be assayed, marked and stamped in such manner as may be ordered. Order in council, October 24, describing the marks to be used.

1906.   Order in council revising marks on foreign plate.

1932.   Gold standards of 15 and 12 karats abolished—14 karat standard introduced.

TABLE OF MARKS

Assay Town	Description	1 Quality
	Gold 22 karat	22
LONDON Established 14th Century	„ 18 „	18
	„ 15 „	15.625
	„ 12 „	12.5
	„ 9 „	9.375
	Silver O.S.	Nil
	„ N.S.	Nil
BIRMINGHAM Established 1773	Gold 22 karat	22
	„ 18 „	18
	„ 15 „	15.625
	„ 12 „	12.5
	„ 9 „	9.375
	Silver O.S.	Nil
	„ N.S.	Nil
CHESTER Re-established 1701	Gold 22 karat	22
	„ 18 „	18
	„ 15 „	15.625
	„ 12 „	12.5
	„ 9 „	9.375
	Silver O.S.	Nil
	„ N.S.	Nil
SHEFFIELD Established 1773	Silver O.S.	Nil
	„ N.S.	Nil
EDINBURGH Established 1457	Gold 22 karat	22
	„ 18 „	18
	„ 15 „	15
	„ 12 „	12
	„ 9 „	9
	Silver O.S.	Nil
	„ N.S.	Britannia
GLASGOW * Established 1819	Gold 22 karat	22
	„ 18 „	18
	„ 15 „	15
	„ 12 „	12
	„ 9 „	9
	Silver O.S.	Nil
	„ N.S.	Britannia
DUBLIN Established 1638. No New Standard silver marked here	Gold 22 karat	22
	„ 20 „	20
	„ 18 „	18
	„ 15 „	15.625
	„ 12 „	12.5
	„ 9 „	9.375
	Silver O.S.	Nil

* The Glasgow Assay Office has used the thistle as an additional

2 Standard	3 Assay Town	4 Date	5 Maker
Crown	Leopard's head without a crown	Letter	Initials
Crown	Leopard's head	Letter	Initials
Nil	Leopard's head	Letter	Initials
Nil	Leopard's head	Letter	Initials
Nil	Leopard's head	Letter	Initials
Lion passant	Leopard's head	Letter	Initials
Britannia	Lion's head erased	Letter	Initials
Crown	Anchor	Letter	Initials
Crown	Anchor	Letter	Initials
Nil	Anchor	Letter	Initials
Nil	Anchor	Letter	Initials
Nil	Anchor	Letter	Initials
Lion passant	Anchor	Letter	Initials
Britannia	Anchor	Letter	Initials
Crown	Sword and 3 sheaves	Letter	Initials
Crown	Sword and 3 sheaves	Letter	Initials
Nil	Sword and 3 sheaves	Letter	Initials
Nil	Sword and 3 sheaves	Letter	Initials
Nil	Sword and 3 sheaves	Letter	Initials
Lion passant	Sword and 3 sheaves	Letter	Initials
Britannia	Sword and 3 sheaves	Letter	Initials
Lion passant	Crown	Letter	Initials
Britannia	Crown	Letter	Initials
Thistle	Castle	Letter	Initials
Thistle	Castle	Letter	Initials
Nil	Castle	Letter	Initials
Nil	Castle	Letter	Initials
Nil	Castle	Letter	Initials
Thistle	Castle	Letter	Initials
Thistle	Castle	Letter	Initials
Lion rampant	Tree, fish, and bell	Letter	Initials
Lion rampant	Tree, fish, and bell	Letter	Initials
Nil	Tree, fish, and bell	Letter	Initials
Nil	Tree, fish, and bell	Letter	Initials
Nil	Tree, fish, and bell	Letter	Initials
Lion rampant	Tree, fish, and bell	Letter	Initials
Lion rampant	Tree, fish, and bell	Letter	Initials
Harp crowned	Hibernia	Letter	Initials
Plume feathers	Hibernia	Letter	Initials
Unicorn's head	Hibernia	Letter	Initials
Nil	Hibernia	Letter	Initials
Nil	Hibernia	Letter	Initials
Nil	Hibernia	Letter	Initials
Harp crowned	Hibernia	Letter	Initials

optional mark since 1914, on silver and gold of 18 and 22 karats.

Assay Town	Description	1 Quality
LONDON Established 14th Century	Gold 22 karat Silver O.S. „ N.S.	... ...
EXETER Re-established 1701	Gold 22 karat Silver O.S. „ N.S.	Leopard's head Leopard's head Lion's head erased
CHESTER Re-established 1701	Gold 22 karat Silver O.S. „ N.S.	Leopard's head Leopard's head Lion's head erased
NEWCASTLE Established 1702	Gold 22 karat Silver O.S. „ N.S.	Leopard's head Leopard's head Lion's head erased
YORK Re-established 1701	Gold 22 karat Silver O.S. „ N.S.	Leopard's head Leopard's head Lion's head erased
NORWICH Re-established 1701	Gold 22 karat Silver O.S. „ N.S.	Leopard's head Leopard's head Lion's head erased
EDINBURGH Re-established 1631	Gold 22 karat Silver O.S. „ N.S.	Assay mark Assay mark Britannia
DUBLIN Re-established 1638	Gold 22 karat Silver O.S.	... ...

2 Standard	3 Assay Town	4 Date	5 Maker
Lion passant	Leopard's head crowned	Letter	Initials
Lion passant	Leopard's head crowned	Letter	Initials
Britannia	Lion's head erased	Letter	Initials
Lion passant	Castle	Letter	Initials
Lion passant	Castle	Letter	Initials
Britannia	Castle	Letter	Initials
Lion passant	3 demi lions and wheatsheaf	Letter	Initials
Lion passant	ditto	Letter	Initials
Britannia	ditto	Letter	Initials
Lion passant	3 castles	Letter	Initials
Lion passant	3 castles	Letter	Initials
Britannia	3 castles	Letter	Initials
Lion passant	5 lions	Letter	Initials
Lion passant	5 lions	Letter	Initials
Britannia	5 lions on a cross	Letter	Initials
Lion passant	Castle and lion	Letter	Initials
Lion passant	Castle and lion	Letter	Initials
Britannia	Castle and lion	Letter	Initials
(*Thistle* in 1759)	Castle	Letter	Initials
...	Castle	Letter	Initials
...	Castle	Letter	Initials
Harp crowned	(*Hibernia* in 1730)	Letter	Initials
Harp crowned	...	Letter	Initials

England

LONDON

By far the most important of the hall marks of Great Britain are, of course, those impressed at Goldsmiths' Hall, London. A large proportion of all the gold and silver plate of the kingdom has always been assayed and marked in the capital. These marks, therefore, must claim our first consideration.

The marks on English plate stamped in London have never been more than five and are now reduced to four, although an additional mark is still placed on all plate of foreign origin assayed in England, as we shall see.

The marks which have been used throughout or at certain periods may be considered in the order in which they were introduced—that is in the following sequence :

    I. The leopard's head
   II. The maker's mark
  III. The annual letter
  IV. The lion passant

I. THE LEOPARD'S HEAD

Taking first the London hall mark of the leopard's head—the "town mark"—which was the earliest assay mark impressed on articles of gold and silver, we shall find that, in the course of five and a half centuries its form has naturally changed.

This mark used to be called sometimes the "liberdes hede," sometimes the "liberd head" and sometimes the "catte's face." The stamp itself was known as the "punson" (a corruption of "puncheon"), and it was always most zealously guarded in the custody of the assay master. The mark is mentioned in the statute of 1300 as "une teste de leopart," and in the charter granted in 1327 to the Goldsmiths' Company, the puncheon of the leopard's head was said even then to have been of ancient use. At all events it is always found on assayed plate from the middle of the fifteenth century. It was most strictly ordained that : "No silver or gold worker should make or sell any silver plate of less fineness than 'sterling' and that it must be assayed and marked with the leopard's head before it is sold."

At first the leopard's head (or lion's head as it has sometimes been called) is crowned. Until early in the sixteenth century it appears in a circular punch and the crown is open. In 1519, however, the crown is closed.

This form was only in use for a short period, 1519 to 1547, when an open crown again is used, within a shaped outline which continues with minute variations until the fourth quarter of the seventeenth century.

In 1678 we have the circular escutcheon again until, in 1697, the introduction of the Britannia standard for silver brought into use the lion's head erased instead of the leopard's head.

The old standard was revived in 1719 and the leopard's head crowned again came into use, but the shield is of very uncertain shape until 1739, when it approximates to that of the date letter in use at the time.

After 1763 the stamp is reduced in size and placed in a plain rounded shield; and so it remained until, in 1822, it was deprived of its ennobling crown and denuded of its mane and beard. This was a drastic and not too happy change from the bold "Henry the Eighth-like" front it had presented in the old punches. It has ever since looked more like the face of a domestic cat than a leopard or lion.

Indeed from the earliest times until 1896 this mark has been constantly changed, and each change has been for the worse. The leopard's head of the present cycle, adopted in 1896, however, certainly is an improvement, though the shield may not meet with universal approval.

II. THE MAKER'S MARK

The maker's mark was first made compulsory in 1336, although it was probably used before that time. The early workers almost invariably employed a symbol or emblem, such as an animal, fish, crown, star or rose. It was ordered that it should be "a

mark of the goldsmith known by the surveyor." In
1378 by an act of Richard II every goldsmith was to
place his own proper mark upon his work and every
piece must bear the mark of the city or borough and
the mark of the assayer "appointed by the king."

In 1423 again the mark or touch of the workman
is insisted on (by an act 2 Henry VI) and yet again
in 1513 (5 Henry VIII). This mark was frequently
a single letter or two letters for the christian or
surname of the maker.

In 1675 an order of the Goldsmiths' Company
enjoins that "the plate workers shall bring their
marks to Goldsmiths' Hall and there strike the same
on a table kept in the assay office and likewise enter
their names and places of habitation in a book there
kept for that purpose, whereby the persons and their
marks may be known unto the wardens of the said
company." In accordance with the act of 1697-8 the
maker was to use the two first letters of his surname
instead of his initials. This enactment compelled a
great number of makers to obtain new punches; but
in 1719 when this act was repealed many makers
returned to their former marks. The matter was
finally settled once and for all by the statutes of
1739 (12 Geo. II), which directed the makers to
destroy the existing punches and to substitute the
initials of their christian and surnames, of entirely
different type from those before used.

Sometimes a small device, such as a cross, star,
etc., is found near the maker's mark. It is the distinctive sign of the workman, used for the purpose of

tracing the work to the actual craftsman who made it. In large workshops some such check is indispensable.

III. THE ANNUAL LETTER

The date mark, sometimes referred to as the assayer's mark, is a letter of the alphabet stamped upon an article with the object of indicating the date of assay. The use of a date letter was introduced at least as early as 1478; since which date the practice has been regularly in use in London. The various alphabets each comprising about twenty letters have succeeded each other, different styles having been used at different times.

At first the letters were used without any shields— the indented shape of the matrix following the outline of the letter—this is called for convenience sake a shaped outline. Since 1560 however the letters have been enclosed in heraldic shields of varying shapes. These coupled with the style of letter used shows, within the limits of twelve months, the date of assay.

Prior to the Restoration the annual date letter was changed on St. Dunstan's Day (May 19) when the new wardens were elected. Since 1660, however, the assay year has commenced on May 30. Each letter thus serves for two halves of two years. The letters J, W, X, Y and Z are omitted in the London lists; sometimes also the letter "U." The provincial towns are by no means so consistent, as a reference to the lists in the following pages will show.

IV. THE LION PASSANT

The standard or quality mark of the lion passant, familiar to all as the mark for English silver, was used on all old standard gold from about 1544 until 1844. Although the first actual mention of " Her Majesty's Lion" is found in the records of the Goldsmiths' Company in 1597, yet it has been found on plate dating from 1545.

The following representations of the lion passant are of those used by the Goldsmiths' Company. The provincial offices vary slightly from these but not materially. The lion was originally represented as passant, guardant, and during the first few years was a fine heraldic beast, crowned and enclosed in an outline following its shape.

From 1548 onwards he is shown uncrowned and was enclosed in a plain rectangle.

For twenty years, 1558-1578, a shaped outline is again employed,

and from 1678 to 1697 was placed in a cartouche with flat base:

Between 1720 and 1739 the lion is again placed in a rectangle, and from that date to 1756 again in a shaped outline. In fact at this period the outline varies. It is an oval in 1784:

but from about this time until 1822 a regular shield of heraldic shape was employed:

From that date on, the lion is not *guardant* :

Since 1896 a somewhat less pleasing outline, tri-lobed above and below, has been in use.

In 1844 the mark for 22 karat gold was changed to the crown and the karat quality 22 given in figures (7 and 8 Vict.). From 1798 (38 Geo. IV) a crown and figures 18 had been used for 18 karat gold though gold of the three lower standards was not allowed until 1854 (17 and 18 Vict.). For these standards numerals alone are used—expressing in decimals the quantity, pure gold being 24 karats.

15 karats = 15.625 on separate stamps.
12   ,,   = 12.5   ,,   ,,   ,,
 9   ,,   = 9.375 ,,   ,,   ,,

In 1932 both the 15 and 12 karat standards were dropped, a new one of 14 karats (14.585) being substituted.

The standard mark for silver was the same as for 22 karat gold until 1697 when the standard was raised to 11 oz. 10 dwts., and "the figure of a woman commonly called Britannia" was ordained and the term "Britannia silver" came into use (25th March, 1697). The Britannia stamp is still used on request for silver of the higher standard, but in 1719 the lower standard was once more permitted, along with the higher, and for this the lion was again employed. It was, as the Act of 1844 sets forth, because of the falsities and frauds committed by dealers in gold and silver works, that the marks were thenceforth differentiated. For the new standard the marks are the figure of Britannia and the lion's head erased, instead of the lion passant and the leopard's head (8 Will. III, 1697). It is worth noting in this connection that Dublin, Glasgow, Edinburgh, Birmingham and Sheffield did not employ the 1697 to 1718 mark for Britannia silver.

V. THE LION'S HEAD ERASED AND FIGURE OF BRITANNIA

When, in 1697, the standard for silver was raised, it was enacted that in lieu of the leopard's head and lion passant, the assay marks should be a lion's head erased and "the figure of a woman commonly called Britannia." This higher standard with these marks continued to be compulsory until 1719 when the old standard was again allowed, with the old marks. The higher standard is still perfectly legal and, when used, is accordingly stamped with the lion's head erased and the figure of Britannia. The present form of these punches is:

VI. THE DUTY MARK

The head of the reigning sovereign in profile indicated that payment of duty had been made. It was impressed at the assay offices on every manufactured article of standard gold and silver which was liable to duty, after payment to the officers of the Goldsmiths' Company, who were appointed receivers.

After the passing of the Duty Act (24 Geo. III, c. 53), which took effect as from St. Dunstan's Day (19th May), 1784, the duty stamp of the *king's head incuse* was used for a short period. We find it in conjunction with the date letters i (1784-5) and k (1785-6), the form being as follows:

The head of George III, from 1786 onward is in an elipse and is in cameo, turned to the right:

This continued of course until the end of his reign —23rd January, 1820.

George IV's head, in use from 1820 to June, 1831, is also facing to the right in the plate mark, although he looks to the left on his coins:

The next sovereign, William IV, was turned to the right in a similar way:

and covers the period 1830 to June, 1837.

The head of Queen Victoria was, however, turned to the left:

This mark continued in use until the year 1890, when the duty being abolished, the mark of the sovereign's head was naturally discontinued.

The duty imposed in 1784 was: on gold eight shillings per ounce; on silver sixpence per ounce. In 1797 while the duty on gold remained the same that on silver was raised to one shilling. In 1804 a further increase took place. The duty on gold was raised to sixteen shillings, silver to one shilling and three pence. Again in 1815 gold rose to seventeen shillings and silver to one shilling and six pence, in addition to the fee for the smith's licence.

On the three lower standards both the *crown* and the sovereign's head *duty mark* were omitted; and, although the same duty was paid on these as on the higher standards, there was no indication of this on the stamps.

VII.   THE MARK FOR FOREIGN PLATE

In 1876, by an Act (39 and 40 Vict. c.35) which made it illegal to sell foreign plate unless it had been assayed and marked at an English assay office, it was enacted that all gold and silver imported from abroad must be thus assayed and stamped with a letter "F" in an escutcheon:

This distinctive stamp was in addition to that of the particular assay office where the mark was impressed. This ordinance continued to be in force until 1904, when a further act was passed, directing that plate brought from foreign parts should be assayed and marked in such manner as His Majesty might by order in council determine.

Following upon this by an order in council made on the 24th October, 1904, published in the London "Gazette" on the 28th of the same month, further regulations were made. In addition to new devices for both gold and silver differing for each assay office the standard had to be denoted.

On foreign gold plate the karat value of the gold had to be shown, together with the karat value in decimals according to the standard:

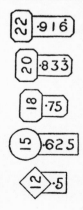

Foreign silver plate had to have the decimal value of the two standards denoted:

The London office mark for gold plate was to be Phœbus Apollo. For gold:

and for silver:

The appropriate marks for provincial offices will be mentioned in their proper places. It may be mentioned here, however, that whatever the device the shield for gold is always the square with cut corners, that for silver an oval.

All the marks specified above continued in use until 1906, when by an order in council made on the 11th May, 1906, and published in the London "Gazette" on the 15th of the same month, further regulations were made in respect of the assaying of foreign plate. It was also found expedient to vary the marks to be used by the assay authorities of

London, Sheffield, Glasgow and Dublin. The marks for Birmingham, Chester and Edinburgh were not altered.

For London, under this order the mark for foreign plate was to be the sign of the constellation Leo; for gold:

and for silver:

Probably a less artistic and more poorly drawn series of hall marks has never been produced than that for foreign plate as promulgated by these two orders.

Cngland

PROVINCIAL ASSAY OFFICES

THE seven towns appointed by the Act of 1423 (2, Hen., VI), were York, Newcastle-upon-Tyne, Norwich, Lincoln, Bristol, Coventry and Salisbury. In these towns mints had already been established and most of them had guilds or fraternities previously existing. The town marks of the first three have been identified, but, as little is known about the "touches" of the remaining four, they probably did not to any considerable extent avail themselves of the privilege of assaying and marking plate.

By the Act of 1700-1 (12 and 13 William III), York, Bristol and Norwich, and in 1701-2, Newcastle-upon-Tyne were re-appointed, with the addition of Exeter and Chester. In these last two cities mints had then lately been instituted for recoining the silver moneys of the kingdom. Coventry, Salisbury and Lincoln had evidently ceased working altogether. Birmingham and Sheffield were not appointed until 1773.

That gold and silver plate were made and stamped in many other towns is of course well known. Of these Barnstaple and Hull are of sufficient importance to be included in the following pages where, for convenience of reference, the towns are arranged in alphabetical order.

BARNSTAPLE

In 1370 the borough records mention Hugh Holbrook, goldsmith, and in the fifteenth century the receiver's accounts refer to a payment to Adrian Goldsmith for repairing the mace. But it is not until the sixteenth century that there is tangible evidence of any considerable manufacture of plate in Barnstaple. In 1571 the town boasted six resident goldsmiths, equal to Bristol and half as many as Exeter. There was probably no chartered guild here, but there was at least a corporate body which took action against defaulting craftsmen.

Though Barnstaple was not an assay town, the early town-mark for plate was a bird in a circle— found on spoons of Elizabethan age with the stamps of Barnstaple makers. This was based upon the early arms of the town. But about 1625 a triple towered castle was adopted as the civic arms and from that time a castle was used as the town mark. In its earlier form it has a prominent gate closed by a portcullis. Later the castle is depicted with the word BARVM (short for Barnstaple). After 1700

the town mark no longer appears. The Act of 12
and 13 William III made it obligatory for goldsmiths to send their plate to a statutory assay office.
Henceforth Barnstaple plate was sent to Exeter for
assay.

Barnstaple's most famous goldsmith was Thomas
Mathew (1563-1611). He did not employ the town
mark, but his own—a flower ornamented with leaves.
No less than twenty chalices said to have been made
by him exist in and around the district. There is
also a fine standing salt by him at the Victoria and
Albert Museum. Other men of the sixteenth and
seventeenth centuries marked their plate with their
names. Among these may be mentioned John
Cotton, Peter Quirk and J. Parnall.

BIRMINGHAM

The history of hall marking at Birmingham starts
with the year 1773. Negative evidence has led to
the belief that until about the middle of the eighteenth century no gold or silver plate of any importance was made there. We have to remember,
however, that not having an assay office of their
own, makers of plate, if any, would have been
obliged to send it either to London or Chester for
assay. It would thus bear no mark to associate it
with Birmingham.

It is known that there were "goldsmiths" (perhaps simply bankers or money-lenders) dwelling in

Birmingham as early as the sixteenth century. But since no records have survived nothing can be stated for certain. Arthur Westwood, assay master, in an informative paper read before the Birmingham and Midland Institute in 1903, has collected much useful information about the manufacture of wrought plate in Birmingham. His researches sustain the belief that until the mid-eighteenth century, such workers in the precious metals as there were, were almost entirely occupied in producing small articles—which were made in great variety. Such articles included jewellery and all manner of knick knacks which could be manufactured without a licence and therefore need not bear a hall mark.

By an Act of Parliament of 1758 all wares in gold not exceeding 2 dwts., or in silver not exceeding 5 dwts., were exempt from the obligation of assay. These were for the most part the wares handled by the toymen, for which Birmingham was famous. But in the quarter century before the passing of the Act of 1773 a certain amount of plate was made " probably the greater part to the order of shopkeepers and others in London to whom it was sold in a nearly finished state . . . and hall marked in London." So we find no less than forty master craftsmen had taken out plate licences before the assay office was established.

Notable among these—indeed the very first to have plate marked by the new office, was Matthew Boulton, who in 1764 set up a factory at Soho, near Birmingham, for the making of solid silver plate.

Not only was he the first to enter silver for assay here but he was also the first to have his work returned—not marked, but deliberately battered out of shape. This was the penalty a maker had to suffer whenever, by accident or design, the quality was not up to standard. Birmingham's first assay master was James Jackson, and the register was opened 31st August, 1773.

The Act of 1773 was passed for the assaying and stamping of wrought silver plate only in Sheffield and Birmingham. Silver goods "shall be marked as followeth: that is to say with the mark of the maker or worker thereof, which shall be the first letter of his christian and surname; and also with the lion passant and with the mark of the company within whose assay office such plate shall be assayed and marked, to denote the goodness thereof, and the place where the same was assayed and marked; and also with a distinct variable mark or letter, which letter or mark shall be annually changed upon the election of new wardens for each company, to denote the year in which such plate is marked."

Sheffield and Birmingham verify their hall marking at the London Mint, and the act required that the assay master shall appear at the Mint annually and verify his proceedings, under a penalty of £200 and dismissal from the office for ever, which is not the case with the other assay offices of Chester, Edinburgh or Dublin.

In the parliamentary inquiry on the subject of hall marks and plate in 1856 it appeared that no other offices save Birmingham and Sheffield had ever within living memory sent up their diet boxes to be tested, being only liable when required to do so. In the parliamentary inquiry of 1879 it was expressly urged that the whole of the assay offices should be placed under the direct supervision of the Mint, so that uniform standard of quality should be guaranteed.

At Birmingham the selection of the variable letter, which is directed to be changed in July, is not confided to any officers, but the custom has been to take the letters in alphabetical order.

By an Act of 1824 (5 Geo. IV) power was given to the company at Birmingham to assay gold as well as silver, and their marks are the same as London, except that the anchor is substituted for the leopard's head.

By the above named Act of 1773, both the officers of Birmingham and Sheffield had jurisdiction to assay and mark all plate made within thirty miles of those towns. By the 17 and 18 of Victoria, all workers or dealers in plate were authorised to register their marks at any assay office legally established which they may select.

The following is the present form of the anchor and the lion passant in use at Birmingham.

The assay mark of Birmingham for foreign plate (order in council, 1904) is an equilateral triangle :

for silver in an oval :

BRISTOL

The details about Bristol are very scanty, although so early as the twelfth century goldsmiths were resident in the city and later there were silver-smiths who sent their goods to Exeter to be assayed. It is not, however, by any means certain that the right of assay was ever freely exercised at Bristol; although it was appointed as an assay town in 1423 and reappointed in 1700.

Indeed, with the exception of one spoon and a milk jug, the only local silver recorded seems to be a stemmed cup, ornamented with punched diamond pattern, in the possession of Lord Elton. From the inscription it appears to have been made in the town although it bears no hall mark. It is late sixteenth century work and bears the inscription :

> " From Mendep I was brought
> Out of a leden mine,
> In Bristol I was wrought
> And now am silver fine."

4

There are some interesting pieces of plate preserved by the Corporation of Bristol, but as these were assayed and marked in London they need not detain us here. No marks that can definitely be associated with Bristol have as yet been recorded.

CHESTER

It appears from the record of Domesday that in the reign of Edward the Confessor there were seven mint masters in Chester. In the reign of Charles I much of the silver was coined here and in that of William II it was one of the six cities in which mints were established for recoining the silver of the kingdom. The mint mark of Chester as found upon the half-crowns of Charles I, struck in 1645, is three *gerbes* or wheat-sheaves.

We have no record of the time when Chester first commenced to assay plate, but it is an ancient hall. It is not mentioned in the statute of the 2nd Henry IV (1423) but an office was probably established here early in the sixteenth century. In an old minute book an entry made before 1573 it is ordained " That noe brother shall delivere noe plate by him wrought unless his touche be marked and set upon the same beffore delivere thereof upon paine of forfeture of everie diffalt to be levied out of his goods iiijs iiijd."

The earliest recorded hall mark, 1665, was based on the ancient city arms—a sword erect between three wheat sheaves. This continued in use until

1697, when the new standard came into use. Since none of the provincial offices was mentioned in the act they were unable to function until the passing of the Act of 1700. By this act Chester was re-appointed and from this time until 1778-9, the town mark was the arms of the city, as adopted in 1580: *three lions passant guardant in pale, dimidiating three garbes.* In 1779-80 they returned for the town mark to the simpler form of the three gerbes and erect sword.

A date letter was in use from year 1701 without interruption, sometimes with the whole alphabet but sometimes finishing with U, V or X. Seventeenth century date letters are not so easily determined.

The only lead we get is from the books of the Chester Goldsmiths' Company, where the first three letters of an alphabet are mentioned, in the years following 1685, in which year a charter from James II was received.

1686. February 1st. And it is further concluded that the warden's marks shall be the coat and crest of the City of Chester on two punsons with a letter for the year.

1687. Paid for ye three punsons . . . 6d.

1690. June 2nd. And the same day the letter was changed from A to B, and so to continue for one year.

1692. April. Paid for a punson and engraving letter C.

1694. Paid Mr. Bullen for a new letter punson.

From this it may be assumed that letter A was in use from 1687 until June of 1690 and letter B from then until 1692. Letter C then comes into use, to be followed by a new letter, presumably D, in 1694. The sequence doubtless continued until, in 1697, the act of William III put an end for the time to the provincial right of assay.

Three hall marks are employed until 1783-4, when the sovereign's head is of course added as duty mark. From 1701 to 1718 the figure of Britannia and the leopard's head erased take the place of the leopard's head crowned and the lion passant.

Chester from year 1889, voluntarily submitted its diet for assay at the Mint, at the same time as the Birmingham and Sheffeld diets were verified.

For foreign plate the Chester assay mark, under the order in council of 1904 was an acorn and two leaves. For gold:

and for silver:

The Chester office closed on August 24, 1962.

EXAMPLES

A porringer, formerly in the possession of *Messrs. Lewis and Son*, Brighton. It shows: 1, the town mark; 2, The city crest—a sword with a bandelet issuing from a crest wreath; 3, the date letter, circa 1690-92; 4, maker's mark, Peter Pemberton.

Spoon with flat stem leaf-shaped end and rat-tail bowl. Date circa 1686-9. *The Earl of Breadalbane.*

Maker's mark for Alexander Pulford. The plume of feathers encircled with a coronet is the badge of the Prince of Wales, who was also Earl of Chester.

EXETER

There are no records pertaining to this hall prior to 1701. The town mark used in the sixteenth and seventeenth centuries (at least as early as 1576 and as late as 1698), was a Roman "X" crowned, with a small star on either side. Usually in a circle, sometimes dotted with pellets, it is sometimes in a shaped outline.

The Act of 1700 re-appointing the city as an assay town came into force on 29th September, 1701. On the 7th August the Company of Goldsmiths met and on the 17th September wardens were appointed.

They resolved, with all convenient speed to put the act into operation and the first assayer was sworn in before the mayor on the 19th November, 1701. The new town mark was to be a triangular castle of three towers (from 1831 to 1837 three separate towers were used in a lozenge form).

The office continued to do useful work until about ninety years ago and a considerable amount of silver assayed here was of Bristol manufacture. Ultimately, however, the amount of business decreased to such an extent that on the 26th June, 1885, a special court was held at the Goldsmiths' Hall. The company resolved, having regard to the small quantity of silver recently marked, that it was not desirable to obtain new punches; and that the premises used for the business should be given up and that no fresh premises should be taken until sufficient applications were received to render it desirable to re-open the hall. The punches were surrendered to the Inland Revenue office, and the books and papers deposited with the solicitor of the company—Mr. Hooper. Six copper plates, on which many of the date letters and makers' marks were preserved are now in the custody of Mr. J. Jerman, of Exeter.

The form of the castle used at Exeter has varied considerably at different times. At first the following form was used :

About 1710 the form was slightly varied:

From 1831 to 1837 the three towers were detached and placed in a rectangle with cut corners:

After that the towers were again joined and this form was retained until the office closed:

The lion passant was very similar to that used at Birmingham:

EXAMPLES

Apostle spoon, circa 1576.—*Messrs. Hancock.*

Spoon. Hexagonal stem, pear-shaped bowl, button top. Date of presentation 1620.—*Earl of Breadalbane.*

Apostle spoon. 1637. *Rev. T. Staniforth.*

   Spoon, circa 1670, with flat stem and oval bowl, with maker's initials W.F.— *Earl of Breadalbane.*

   Split-head spoon, pricked
EP
   1689.—*Messrs. Ellett*
MN
   Lake and Son.

     Tankard. Date letter 1703. *Ibid.*

    Tankards of new standard. Date letter for 1703.— *Messrs. Hancock.*

      Salver, circa 1710.—*Messrs. Ellett Lake and Son.*

Split head spoon. Date
letter for 1711.—*Ibid.*

Rat tail spoon. Date letter
for 1712. Maker's mark
of Peter Eliot of Dart-
mouth.—*Messrs. Han-
cock.*

HULL

Although there is no documentary evidence to
point to the antiquity of the goldsmiths' craft at
Kingston upon Hull, there are sufficient extant
examples of local plate to show that, at least during
the seventeenth century, the making and marking
of plate was continuous in the town.   There was
never a properly constituted assay office here, however, and it would seem, since there is much varia-
tion in the town mark, that each maker probably
had his own punch.

The earliest mark employed was a capital H, for
Hull.   Later this was used with another punch of
the arms of the town—*three ducal crowns in pale*,
and still later the three crowns in a shield were

employed alone. For a short time, too, a date letter was in use though only a few letters (E-H) have been identified.

EXAMPLE

     Spoon. Date circa 1660.

LINCOLN

This city was mentioned as an assay town in the Act of 1423, but there is little surviving plate which can definitely be ascribed to a Lincoln origin. The arms of the city are *argent, on a cross gules, a fleur de lis or*, and the following may be taken as examples of Lincoln marks.

     A rat tail spoon, circa 1660.— *The Rev. T. Staniforth.*

    A piece of plate, seventeenth century.—*Messrs. Hancock.*

NEWCASTLE

At Newcastle-upon-Tyne as early as 1249, Henry III commanded the bailiffs and good men to choose four of the most prudent and trusty men of their town for the office of moneyers there, and other four like persons for keeping the King's Mint in that town; also, two fit and prudent goldsmiths to be assayers of the money to be made there.

The Act of 1423 included Newcastle as one of the assay towns and, at that date, if not before, there were probably sufficient workers in the craft to have formed a fraternity. A century later, in 1536, their guild was amalgamated with that of the plumbers and glaziers and the united company were required to go together, on the feast of Corpus Christi to maintain their play of the "Three Kings of Coleyn." They were to have four wardens and they had their hall in "Maden Tower" granted to them in 1619.

In spite of such evidence of corporate activity it seems probable that little plate was assayed here during this period, for the earliest piece extant cannot be dated earlier than the third quarter of the seventeenth century.

No date letter was in use at this time, approximate dates can therefore be obtained only from inscriptions or makers' marks. The Act of William III, in 1696, by which the standard was raised and the provincial offices deprived of the right of assay, was rectified by the Act of 1700. For some unaccountable reason Newcastle was left out on this occasion and was only reinstated by a special act in the following year. Thus it was not until 1702 that a date letter was instituted.

The town mark was subjected to slight variations. From about 1658 to about 1670 a single castle was used in a straight-pointed shield.

From thence onwards it was always three castles, two above and one below, in shields of varying shapes as follows:

From circa 1670 to circa 1684:

From about 1684 to about 1696:

From that date until 1702 two types of shield are found:

From 1702 to 1728:

From 1728 to about 1757 the heart shape was used again—from then to 1800 an oviform:

Referring to the table of date letters, it will be seen that, from 1702 when first employed they are fairly regular, with certain exceptions. In the first cycles the letter M, for 1712 appeared when one would expect it to be for 1714, but that it was used for 1712 is shown by a paten possessed by Sherburn Hospital, which bears the inscription, "Ex dono Anno 1712." That letter may therefore have been used for more than one year.

In 1719-20 and 1720-21 we have "D" and "E" repeated. In cycle 4, after the italic capital "B" there would seem to have been no letter employed until 1769-70 when the italic "C" is used. There is no explanation of this hiatus in the minute books.

At one period the Newcastle office is alleged to have assayed as much as 12,500 ounces per annum. But gradually its work fell off and it was finally closed in 1884.

EXAMPLES

A porringer with two handles, fluted base and g a d r o o n e d band at top. Circa 1680.—*The Earl of Breadalbane.*

Large gravy ladle. Date letter 1722-3. —*A. Attenborough Esq.*

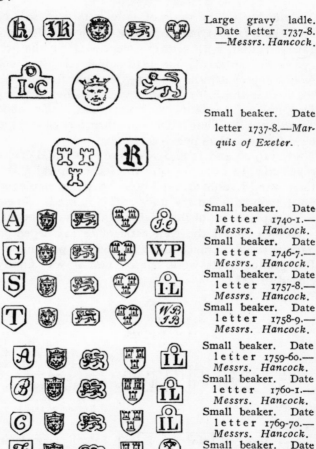

Large gravy ladle. Date letter 1737-8. —*Messrs. Hancock.*

Small beaker. Date letter 1737-8.—*Marquis of Exeter.*

Small beaker. Date letter 1740-1.— *Messrs. Hancock.*

Small beaker. Date letter 1746-7.— *Messrs. Hancock.*

Small beaker. Date letter 1757-8.— *Messrs. Hancock.*

Small beaker. Date letter 1758-9.— *Messrs. Hancock.*

Small beaker. Date letter 1759-60.— *Messrs. Hancock.*

Small beaker. Date letter 1760-1.— *Messrs. Hancock.*

Small beaker. Date letter 1769-70.— *Messrs. Hancock.*

Small beaker. Date letter 1772-3.— *Messrs. Hancock.*

NORWICH

In the ancient city of Norwich, as one would expect of so historic a town, gold and silver plate has been produced from very early times. It was one of the seven provincial assay towns appointed by the Act of 1423; but, as early records disclose, there was already a flourishing guild of goldsmiths here during the preceding two centuries.

The marking of Norwich plate does not however seem to have been insisted upon officially, nor was any attempt made to regularise it until the middle of the 16th century.

In the year 1564 a petition was presented to the Corporation, showing that up to that time "no common stampp or marke have thereto been used and occupied within the said cittie whereby the said works of sylver . . . might be stamped and signed." It was therefore ordained that "from and after the date of this assembly every artificer . . . shall trewly and faithfully worke according to trewth and honestie," and that "the standerde towching the fynes of sylver, whereby the said artificers at all times hereafter shall worke all their works of sylver within the said cittie and suburbes of the same shall be accepted, reputed and taken to be of souche and the same fynes and goodnes and better as the standerde of the lyberds hedde with the crowne" (i.e., of the London standard) "and that a comon stampp or towche of the arms or ensigne of the said

cittie, beying the castell and the lyon, shall be
provided to remayne in the custody and keeping of
the wardens of the said art."

From another early Norwich document, "The
Oath of the Stranger Goldsmiths" (undated but
contemporary with this), we learn that the gold was
to be as good "as the alaye of the iiijth and the
silver as good as the money of the King." The
"alaye of the iiijth" was six karats of alloy to the
ounce of 24 karats. This standard had been in use
from 1477 in lieu of the "alaye" of the fifth (the
touch of Paris), and it continued in force until 1575.
The standard for silver—18 dwts. alloy to the 12
ounce pound—had been adopted so early as 1300.

Norwich would seem to have assayed plate up to
the beginning of the eighteenth century since on July
1, 1702, one Robert Hartstonge, was sworn in as
assayer. But, since no date letter was used between
1585 and 1624 it has been suggested by Jackson that
between those dates the plate was sent to London
for assay.

In addition to the town mark of the castle and lion
another assay mark is found on some Norwich plate.
This is a Tudor rose crowned and the two marks
were sometimes used together. This second mark,
shown by the "Oath of the Assay Master" to have
been an official Norwich mark has always been
somewhat of a puzzle. The most probable explanation of its use has been advanced by Mr. H. D. Ellis,
in "The Burlington Magazine," XII, 363. His
suggestion is that it may have been prescribed to

denote the work of the stranger and alien craftsmen of the city. This stamp of the rose crowned is frequently met with on plate of the sixteenth century and before the Commonwealth—at a time when a numerous Dutch colony had taken refuge in the city. The origin of Norwich or "Dordrecht" beakers is still debated. Heer Voet maintains that the marks are Dutch, but even if the rose crowned was introduced from Holland, it is probable that its use was restricted to the Dutch guild working in Norwich.

An annual date letter came into use in 1565 but its employment would appear to have been irregular. Of the first cycle, presumed to be of twenty years, only nine certain letters are on record. One of these, the Roman capital "D" (with the town mark and the orb and cross), is recorded on a gilt cylindrical salt and cover, elaborately chased with strap-work and elegant borders. It bears the inscription: "The Gyfte of Peter Reade, Esquiar, to the Corporation." This treasure of the corporation plate was therefore made and stamped in 1568. Peter Reade died that year. The letter "C" is given to us on an Elizabethan cup belonging to Barsham, 1567-8.

A silver mounted coco-nut cup in the Victoria and Albert Museum bears the crowned rose, the maker's mark, a star, and a date letter R. Since it bears a date, 1576, on the coco-nut the date of the silver work must be somewhat later. Presuming an unbroken cycle of date letters "R" would give the date 1581-2. Jackson queries its Norwich origin,

5

without any justification.

Among the corporation plate is a gilt tazza on short baluster stem. Engraved round the rim in cusped letters is the inscription: THE + MOST + HEREOF + IS + DVNE + BY + PETER + PETERSON. It was exhibited at South Kensington in the 1862 Exhibition. Peterson was the most eminent goldsmith of his time in Norwich. Born about 1518, he became freeman in 1554, chamberlain of the city in 1574 and died in 1603. The tazza bears two marks —the town mark and the orb and cross. The latter is said to be a maker's mark, but it was not that of Peterson, which was a sun.

The mark reproduced from the chalice at Diss Church, 1565-6, provides a further interesting feature worthy of note. This is the herringbone-like mark about half an inch long. This is the gouged assay mark, found in the sixteenth and early seventeenth centuries, only on certain Norwich and Scottish plate, though it was used also on the Continent. It is apparently another link with the Dutch refugees of the period. It occurs again on the chalice at Booton, with date letter "C" for 1567-8; a chalice which after being stolen in 1919 was bought in the Caledonian Market for four pounds and later returned to its original home. It also is found on two "Dordrecht" beakers exhibited at the How Exhibition in 1936, one of which bears the Norwich date letter for 1626, the other for 1635.

EXAMPLES

Chalice. Date letter for 1565-6.—*Diss Church.*

Cup. Date letter for 1567-8. — *B a s h a m Church.*

Communion cup of same date. — *Messrs Hancock.*

Silver gilt salt. Date letter for 1568-9.—*Norwich Corporation.*

 ★ R

Mount of a coco-nut cup. Date letter R (1581).— *The Victoria and Albert Museum.*

Seal-top spoon. Date letter for 1636-7.—*J. H. Walter, Esq.*

Split head spoon. Circa 1662. Probably by Arthur Heaslewood.—*J. H. Walter, Esq.*

Tankard. Date letter for 1691-2. By Thomas H a v e r s. — *J a m e s Reeve, Esq.*

Beaker. Date letter for 1697-8.—*J. H. Walter, Esq.*

SHEFFIELD

An assay office was instituted at Sheffield by the same Act of Parliament (of 1773) as that by which Birmingham was empowered to assay.

The town mark is a crown, which is sometimes combined on the same punch as the date letter. The same thing occurs with regard to the lion passant and crown. Generally, however, they are found as separate stamps.

Mr. B. W. Watson, assay master, kindly furnished a list of the date letters for Major Markham's sixth edition, from their commencement in 1773. The minute books record the letter chosen for each succeeding year—the change takes place on the first Monday in July. Were it not for such a record it might have been difficult to construct the cycle letters, for the plan adopted at Sheffield differed, up to 1824, from that of all other offices. Instead of taking the alphabet in regular order, the letter for each year was chosen at random. After 1824, however, the normal sequence of the alphabet was used.

The forms of the lion passant and crown were formerly :

But with the commencement of cycle 7 in 1918 they were placed in a straight pointed shield, to match the escutcheons of the date letters :

The Sheffield mark for foreign plate, under the 1904 order in council, was crossed arrows with a bar for gold :

and for silver :

The order of 1906 substituted for this the sign of libra, for gold :

and for silver :

EXAMPLES

Candlestick. Date letter for 1791-2.—*J. H. Walter, Esq.*

Salver. Date letter for 1831-2. — *W. Shoesmith, Esq.*

YORK

York is one of the most ancient cities in England and over a thousand years ago a mint was established within its walls. There were gold and silversmiths here in the thirteenth century and it was one of the towns appointed to assay by the Act of 1423. Even earlier than that, however, York was of sufficient importance to have had its own mark and for that mark to have been referred to in 1412 as "le comune touch de la cite."

This early mark is surmised to have been a double rose, within a treasure of arches and beaded circle, but at least so early as the time of Queen Elizabeth the town mark is described as "the half-

leopard's head and half fleur de lys." The conjunction of the lis and the rose it has been suggested
is an allusion to the union of the rival houses of
York and Lancaster by the marriage of Henry VII
to the Princess Margaret, daughter of Edward IV,
in 1486.

There would appear to be five variants of this
punch. The first used until 1569, the second only
found on communion cups of 1570 and 1571, though
it may have been used later. A third is identified
first in 1583 and continues in use until 1624, a fourth
begins with 1625 and ends at 1697, while the fifth
continues from 1680 to 1697 when the act of that
year suspended the powers of assay. The differenti-
ation of these is difficult, even for the specialist and
is often made more so by the imperfect way in which
the punches have been impressed.

After the re-establishment of the right of assay in
1700, the town mark was ordained to be the arms of
the city—in a shield on a cross five lions passant
guardant. This remained the recognised York
mark until the office was finally closed in 1856.
Often enough, however, the mark was omitted.

The use of the date letter may be summarised as
follows:

1560 to 1583. Roman capitals in variously shaped
shields—omitting J and U.
1583 to 1607. Black letter, small, in pointed shields.
1607 to 1631. Old English capitals—shields similar.
1631 to 1657. Small italics—shields similar.
1657 to 1682. Script capitals—shields similar.

1682 to 1698.   Black letter—shields similar.

1700 to 1714.   Capitals A to O with Britannia.

1714 to 1787.   (No regular cycles. Not much business would seem to have been done.)

1787 to 1812.   Cycles resumed with king's head, duty mark.

1812 to 1837.   Small black letter.

1837 to 1857.   Roman capitals.

In 1848 we find it mentioned as an assay town, but as doing very little business. The last duty paid at the Inland Revenue Office was in July, 1869.

The corporation of the city possesses some interesting pieces of plate. A state sword with velvet scabbard, mounted in silver, bears the arms of the city, the arms of Bowes, etc., of the time of Henry VIII. On the blade is this inscription: " SYR MARTYN BOWES KNIGHT, BORNE WITHIN THIS CITIE OF YORK AND MAIOR OF THE CITIE OF LONDON 1545. FOR A REMEMBRANCE." On the other side: " GAVE THIS SWORD TO THE MAIOR AND COMMUNALTIE OF THIS SAID HONORABLE CITIE."

Two tankards, the gift of Thomas Bawtrey in 1673, engraved with the arms of York, were made at York and stamped with the York mark and the italic capital P.

A silver cup and paten belonging to the church of Chapel-Allerton, Leeds, has three marks: a half fleur-de-lis and half rose crowned; an italic b, similar to the London date letter of 1619; and the maker's initials R.H. On the rim is the date of presentation 1633.

A stoneware jug has in relief the royal arms of England and the date 1576. It is mounted in silver and bears three stamps: that of the maker, the half lis and rose and the date letter R (1575-6). It is in Mr. Addington's collection.

EXAMPLES

Apostle spoon. Date letter for 1644-5. — *Dallington Church, Northampton-shire.*

Apostle spoon. Date letter for 1626.—*Rev. T. Stani-forth.*

A piece of plate, seventeenth century.—*Messrs Hancock.*

A piece of plate, seventeenth century.—*Messrs Hancock.*

Spoon with flat stem, leaf-shaped end and oval bowl. Date letter for 1693,—*Earl of Breadalbane.*

An oval engraved silver tea-pot. Eighteenth century. —*Messrs. Hancock.*

Scotland

EDINBURGH

THE assay office here dates from the year 1457 and from that time until 1483 two marks only were used. One of these was the mark of the maker—formerly some simple device, with or without the maker's initials, or, at a later period, the initials of his christian and surname. The other:

THE STANDARD MARK

was that of the deacon of the craft—a monogram. This continued to be used until in 1681 it was superseded by that of the assay master. Finally the present standard mark of the thistle was introduced in 1759. This standard mark was applied to both gold and silver (for gold with the "22" or "18" to denote the two higher standards). The figure of Britannia was of course added for the new standard silver when employed. The present mark is:

Burns, in his "Old Scottish Communion Plate," gives a list of deacon's marks which are important in fixing the date of pieces before 1681.

THE TOWN MARK

The Edinburgh town or hall mark, based upon the arms of the city—a castle with three towers—was referred to in an act of James II (of Scotland) in 1457 and alluded to again in the acts of 1483 and 1555. At least ten different types of castles have been used at various times, that at present in use being :

THE DATE MARK

The date letter introduced in 1681, was changed at the first hall day of October in each year and the cycles follow a regular sequence.

FOREIGN PLATE

Under the order in council of 1904 foreign plate assayed at Edinburgh was to be marked with the St. Andrew's Cross. For gold :

and for silver :

EXAMPLES

 Mark given in Mr. J. H. Sanderson's paper "Trans. Soc. Antiq. Scotland, IV," p. 543 and pl. XX. Mark of George Robertson, maker of the city mace. Deacon's mark George Cranford. Ca. 1615-23.

 On the Dalkeith church plate. Deacon's mark James Fairbairne. Ca. 1551-63.

 Plate belonging to Trinity College Church, Edinburgh, bearing the date 1663. Deacon's mark George Cranford. Ca. 1615-23.

 A quaigh, with hemispherical bowl and flat, projecting handles, one of which bears A.C., the other I.Mc L. Engraved outside with full blown roses and lilies. Date letter for 1713-4. — *Earl of Breadalbane*.

 Tablespoon of French pattern, rat's tail. Date letter for 1749-50.—*Earl of Breadalbane*.

 A dessert spoon of French pattern. Date letter for 1759-60.

 Spoon in possession of *Earl of Breadalbane*. Date letter for 1766-7.

Spoon.   Date letter for
1760-1.—*J. P. Stott,
Esq.*

GLASGOW

In early days the Glasgow goldsmiths were linked
with the hammermen whose combined trades were
incorporated by a seal of cause granted by the town
council in 1536.   During the succeeding century it
seems likely that the craft was in a fairly flourishing
condition.

The town mark then, as now, was the most
intricate of any hall mark ever used by any town.
It was based on the city arms and consisted of an
oak tree with a hand bell hanging from its branches
on one side, a bird on the top branch, and across the
trunk a salmon with a ring in its mouth.

The ancient marks on plate were: (1) this town
mark; (2) the maker's mark (his initials—frequently
repeated); and (3) a date letter.   Up to the present
it has only been possible to assign correct dates for
very few years.   The earliest dated piece—a communion cup at Hamilton—has the date letter "Q"
in old English (for 1696-7).   The first cycle would
therefore seem to have been introduced in 1681-2.
A second cycle, beginning in 1706-7, of roman
capitals followed.   A new series commenced with
the latest assay office charter, granted in 1819 (59

Geo. III, c. 28). The enactment covered the city of Glasgow and forty miles around. All plate made within this radius was therefore to be assayed and marked at the Glasgow office.

The lion rampant is the standard mark for both gold and silver—except 9 karat gold. Both gold and silver also bear the town mark and date letter. In addition the duty mark was, of course, used up to 1890 and for the higher standard silver (·959) the figure of Britannia. These, with the mark of the maker make the full complement.

The Scottish Act of 6 and 9 Wm. IV in some respects extended to Glasgow, although the craft is generally regulated by the 59 Geo. III. The latter statute (1836) recommended the thistle as the standard mark, but they continued to use the lion rampant. The lower standards of fifteen, twelve and nine karat gold bear the marks 15-·625, 12-·5 and 9-·375.

The mark for foreign plate, under the order in council of 1904 was, for gold a bishop's mitre :

and for silver :

This was altered by the order of 1906 to a double
sans-serif letter "F" inverted in shields of the
same two shapes

The Glasgow office closed in 1964.

EXAMPLES

Tazza, chased with leaf
scrolls, bordered with
engrailed lines. The
work is evidently of the
time of Charles II.
1670-80. — *Messrs. Han-
cock.*

An oval silver box, made to
contain the wax seal of a
diploma granted by the
University. Ca. 1776-80.
Maker's mark, probably
meant to be M & C (for
Milne and Campbell, who
had a shop in Glasgow
about 1776). — *Earl of
Breadalbane.*

Sugar castor, chased with
festoons of roses. Late
XVIIIth century. (The
letter S was used presum-
ably as a standard mark
on Scottish plate between
1717 and about 1800.)

SCOTTISH PROVINCIAL MARKS

ABERDEEN

Apart from Edinburgh and Glasgow there were goldsmiths following their trade in many other important towns—in fact, the making of plate was hardly at all restricted until, in 1836, an act of Parliament definitely limited the power of assay to the two principal cities. Prior to that the burghs would seem to have had the power to make their own arrangements. Thus Aberdeen in 1649, appointed a "tryar" and decided upon a town mark, but after a short time it would appear that each maker used a punch of his own.

The town arms—three towers triple towered—was used as the town mark for a short time in the eighteenth century. But the mark adopted by the assay office consisted of two or more of the letters of the name Aberdeen. Thus the letters ABD, with the mark of contraction above, or later ABDN, as in the following :

EXAMPLES

Tablespoon, handle turned up and ridges on the front of the stem. Ca. 1780.—*Earl of Breadalbane.*

72

 Small caddy spoon. Ca. 1880.—
W. K. Macdonald, Esq.

ARBROATH

The arms of this burgh are a portcullis beneath a wreath of laurel and this portcullis was used as a hall mark on the silver worked at this place.

EXAMPLE

 A fork, with shell pattern. Ca. 1880.
—*W. K. Macdonald, Esq.*

BANFF

The mark used at Banff varied a great deal, but it generally consisted of the name of the town or some contraction thereof. It is seldom difficult to recognise.

EXAMPLES

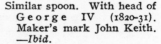 Dessert spoon of French pattern.—*Earl of Breadalbane.*

 Similar spoon. With head of G e o r g e IV (1820-31). Maker's mark John Keith. —*Ibid.*

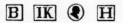 Tablespoon. Same maker.— *Ibid.*

Similar spoon. Same maker with king's head.—*Ibid.*

DUNDEE

There were goldsmiths working here from the sixteenth century.

The town mark adopted by the assay office was based, as in so many other cases, upon the arms of the town—a pot with two handles containing three lilies—as shown in the following:

EXAMPLES

On a pair of sugar tongs, shell and fiddle pattern. Ca. 1880. —*Earl of Breadalbane*.

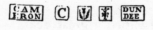

Tablespoon, rat's tail, flat stem, leaf-shaped end. 1730. —*Ibid*.

Teaspoon, fiddle head. Nineteenth century.—*Ibid*.

Small spoon. Nineteenth century.—*W. K. Macdonald, Esq*.

ELGIN

Like the towns of Aberdeen, Inverness and Banff, which adopted abbreviations of their names, Elgin used the contraction ELN. Two other stamps are also found used as hall marks however. One was a view of the west front of Elgin Cathedral, the other the figure of St. Egidius (St. Giles), the patron

saint of Elgin. All known examples of plate with
the Elgin mark are of late date.

EXAMPLE

On a table spoon with oval
bowl, the end of the handle
turned upward with
a ridge down the centre.
Ca. 1730-60. Here the
figure of St. Egidius
occurs with the ELN.—
Earl of Breadalbane.

GREENOCK

Several marks were used in this burgh. Sometimes a ship in full sail, sometimes an anchor and
sometimes a green oak. All these marks may be
found on a single article.

EXAMPLES

Five teaspoons. French pattern, eighteenth century.—
Earl of Breadalbane.

Teaspoon and tongs. French
pattern, eighteenth century.
—*Ibid.*

Caddy spoon, with a shell-shaped bowl, fiddle head,
with the Scottish standard
mark. Ca. 1820.—*Ibid.*

A Scottish brooch, with circular broad band, plain of surface, with hinge and clasp at
back.—*Ibid.*

INVERNESS

There have been goldsmiths in this town since the middle of the seventeenth century. The mark generally used was INS, as a short form of the name of the town. A dromedary or a cornucopia—one of the supporters of the arms and the crest of the town —were sometimes employed.

EXAMPLES

A teaspoon, fiddle head. Ca. 1820. (With the cornucopia.)—*Earl of Breadalbane.*

A large annular Scottish brooch, flat, with engraved vandykes and a cluster of fine small annulets between each. This shows the dromedary town mark, as well as the INS. Also the deacon's mark, attributed to Charles Jamison. Ca. 1810.— *Ibid.*

MONTROSE

This burgh royal, in allusion to its name and the arms, uses a rose, sometimes a double rose, as its town mark. It is placed either in a shield or a circle.

PERTH

Goldsmiths have been established in this city from early times. In the seventeenth century the town mark was the paschal lamb bearing the banner of St. Andrew, taken from the city arms: An eagle displayed with two heads or, surmounted on the breast with an escutcheon gules, charged with the holy lamb, passant regardant, carrying the banner of St. Andrew.

Somewhat later the double-headed eagle displayed came into use and continued to be used until the beginning of the 19th century.

EXAMPLES

A small quaigh or cup with two handles, date ca. 1660.—*C. A. North, Esq.*

A split-head spoon, ca. 1675.—*J. H. Walters, Esq.*

Set of table spoons, French pattern with rat tail, date about 1760.— *Earl of Breadalbane.*

A dessert spoon, fiddle head, ca. 1820. Maker's mark of Robert Kay (recorded as silversmith at Perth in 1815).—*Earl of Breadalbane.*

Set of four salt cellars, gadrooned edges, three claw legs. Ca. 1810.—*Ibid.*

STIRLING

The only mark found upon silver which can be assigned to this town is a castle, triple towered without windows, in an irregular shield.

An oblong tobacco box, engraved on the cover with two coats of arms, surmounted by a ducal coronet. The town mark here has the letter "S" to distinguish it from the castle of Edinburgh. The maker's mark is a mermaid and star with his initials G.B.—*Earl of Breadalbane.*

TAIN

This Ross-shire town used as town mark the name in capitals as in the following:

EXAMPLE

A pair of toddy ladles, about 1800.—*Earl of Breadalbane.*

Ireland

DUBLIN

The Goldsmiths' Company of Dublin has for a long time had the exclusive management of the assaying and marking of wrought gold and silver plate in Ireland.

The records of the Company have survived nearly intact and are more complete than those of any Goldsmiths' Company of England or Scotland. The Company's Charter together with lists of masters, wardens, journeymen and apprentices covering most of its existence have been published in Jackson's *English Goldsmiths and their Marks*, 2nd edition 1921.

There were goldsmiths working here in the 12th century and a goldsmith guild had been established by royal charter long prior to the charter of 1637.

It is recorded that in April, 1557, the Goldsmiths' Corporation appealed to the city assembly for leave to bring in a copy of their charter, which had been burnt. Again in September of that year they petitioned that none should exercise the art unless admitted by the master and warden and that none should be so admitted unless he were of English name and blood and a freeman.

The corporation archives under the date 1605 record a complaint made about abuses which had arisen. Goldsmiths were evidently making a considerable amount of base or corrupt silver. The council thereupon ordered that every goldsmith should have a special mark. The mayor and constable of the staple were to be the assay masters and the special mark was to be the figure of a lion, a harp and a castle.

No plate with this mark is known. The earliest mark we have is the harp. It was possibly used before the charter of Charles I, by which the old company obtained incorporation (13 Chas. I, 1637). This enactment provided that the mark of the harp crowned should be used only for 22 karat gold and the 11 oz. 2 dwt. standard silver.

Thus "the harp crowned" used in various forms throughout the years

became the

STANDARD MARK.

It has continued in use ever since in accordance with this ordinance, reinforced by the Plate Assay Amendment Act, 1931. An Act of 1784 ordained that gold of 20 karats (a standard peculiar to Ireland) was to be marked with a plume of three feathers and the figure 20; gold of 18 karats with a unicorn's head and 18. The lower standards of 15, 12 and 9 karats, introduced in the mid 19th century and later restricted to 14 and 9 karats, were marked 15.625, 14.585, 12.5 and 9.375 respectively. No silver of Britannia standard has been made in Ireland, but foreign silver of this standard is marked 9584.

THE DUTY MARKS

The figure of Hibernia, used on gold and silver of all standards, was introduced in 1730-1 as a tax mark. From 1807 to 1890, the English tax mark of the reigning monarch's head was added. The latter mark is not usually found on gold since most pieces of jewellery were exempt.

The form and shield shape of the Hibernia and the Harp punches accompanying the date letters vary considerably from alphabet to alphabet and even within the same alphabet especially in the late 18th and early 19th centuries. For accurate dating of Irish silver and gold, account must be taken of these changes which follow a pattern not yet entirely known. Since 1784, the Hibernia and Harp punches for gold are quite different from those for silver.

THE MAKER'S MARK

The maker's mark in Ireland, as elsewhere, was formerly some distinctive device with or without the initials of the goldsmith. Later the initials of his christian and surname were used.

THE DATE LETTER

Dated examples of Dublin plate are rare before 1690. From 1638, the year in which the communion flagon was given by Moses Hill to Trinity College, Dublin, the fact is established, confirmed also by the charter granted by Charles I, December 22, 1637, that a roman letter was adopted, commencing for that year with A. Letters B, C, D, I, S and T of this alphabet have been recorded.

The following four letters have been noted from the next alphabet:

Then in 1679 several pieces have been found with an old English B from the following cycle. The sequence was irregular during the war period of 1688-93. In 1693 the old English cycle continues with the letter K, reaching Z in 1716-7. With 1717-8 a court-hand alphabet starts, but after the first three letters a fresh alphabet was started (1720-1) and, omitting J, ran right through, after which roman alphabets are used for a whole century.

FOREIGN PLATE

The assay mark for foreign plate, chosen under the order in council of 1904, was a shamrock leaf, for gold:

and for silver:

By the later order of 1906 this was changed to the heraldic bouget (mediaeval vessel for carrying water, formed by two leather pouches attached to a crossbar or yoke):

In 1921, 26 of the 32 counties of Ireland received Dominion status as the Irish Free State, a name later changed to the Republic of Ireland after leaving the British Commonwealth.

In 1927 and 1931, the Republic passed legislation on assaying which provided for continuation of the existing types of marks on silver and gold of Irish manufacture and for extension of the use of the punches for foreign wares instituted in 1906 to cover also those made in the United Kingdom.

JUBILEE MARK

This mark was applied during the year 1966 to all Irish gold and silver, other than jewellery and watch cases, in addition to the normal hallmark.

Captain Ronald Le Bas, Assay Master, provided valuable information on the Irish assay offices.

EXAMPLES

 Two tankards presented in 1680 to the Guild of St. John. Date 1680.—*Merchant Taylors' Company.*

 Piece of plate. Date 1724-5. —*Messrs. Hancock.*

 Mace, dated 1728, the top embossed with the royal arms.—*Messrs. Hancock.*

 A two-handled cup. Date 1739-40. — *Messrs. Hancock.*

 Silver-gilt sugar sifter. Date 1787-8.—*J. H. Walter, Esq.*

Spoon. Date 1804.— *J. P. Stott, Esq.*

CORK

Cork never employed a date letter and before 1656 no distinctive marks were impressed upon the plate made here. In the year mentioned, however, the goldsmiths were formerly incorporated and from this time on a maker's mark is usually employed— initials or some device. A town mark, too, is not infrequently found during the rest of the century, while from the beginning of the 18th century the town mark is always present on important pieces.

This town mark varies. The early mark based on the city arms was a ship in full sail between two castles—sometimes on separate stamps. But sometimes only one castle is shown or two castles without the ship.

About 1715, however, the word STIRLING (STAR-LING or STER) supersedes and up to about 1800 this and the maker's initials are the only marks employed. After this we find the Cork marks used with the Dublin punches for a few years, Dublin marks replacing them entirely by about 1815.

LIMERICK

A fair quantity of silver was made in Limerick during the second half of the 18th century. A little earlier, a town mark of a two-towered castle gateway was used, soon replaced by a punch of the word STERLING, variously spelt, together with the maker's initials. Use of the STERLING punch was discontinued in the early 19th century, most work being taken to Dublin for hallmarking.

GALWAY

Small quantities of plate were marked here in the first half of the 18th century. The town mark of an anchor—all too commonly used by other seaports throughout Europe—was employed, accompanied by a punch of the maker's initials.

KINSALE

A few pieces of plate are tentatively attributed to this town, but they bear a maker's mark only and belong to the early 18th century. At this period there was a flourishing Company of Blacksmiths in the town, and it included associated trades, mentioning silversmiths specifically.

NEW GENEVA

No gold or silver has ever been traced to this settlement in Co. Waterford set up by Statute in 1784 to house Swiss protestant immigrants including mainly watchmakers. The settlement failed almost at once, the special hallmarks provided for it in the Statute apparently never having been used.

BELFAST

The marks of a 'hand' once attributed to Belfast as the red hand of Ulster are now known to come from Malta during the period of the Napoleonic wars. No other marks have been traced to the then small town of Belfast.

YOUGHAL

Some plate was made and stamped here, the goldsmiths having been incorporated with the hammermen by charter of 1657. The town mark was the civic arms: a lymphad* within variously shaped outlines.

---

* A single masted sailing boat or yawl, rebus of the name of the town.

JUBILEE MARK

Voluntary mark applied to silver only 1933-4, 1934-5 and 1935-6 to commemorate the Silver Jubilee of King George and Queen Mary in 1935.

CORONATION MARK

Voluntary mark applied to gold and silver wares assayed between 1 October 1952 and 31 December 1953 to commemorate the coronation of Queen Elizabeth II.

7

SUMMARY OF TOWN MARKS

London

Birmingham

Chester

Exeter

Newcastle

Norwich

Sheffield

York

Edinburgh

Glasgow

Dublin

90

TOWN MARKS FOR IMPORTED WARES
(since 1906)

	Silver	Gold
London		
Birmingham		
Chester		
Sheffield		
Edinburgh		
Glasgow		
Dublin		

DATES OF ACCESSION OF THE SOVEREIGNS

Henry VII	1485
Henry VIII	1509
Edward VI	1547
Mary	1553
Elizabeth I	1558
James I	1603
Charles I	1625
Commonwealth	1649
Charles II	1660
James II	1685
William & Mary	1689
William III	1695
Anne	1702
George I	1714
George II	1727
George III	1760
George IV	1820
William IV	1830
Victoria	1837
Edward VII	1901
George V	1910
Edward VIII	1936
George VI	1936
Elizabeth II	1952

TABLES OF DATE LETTERS

LONDON

From

1477 1. Leopard's Head crowned. 2. Date Letter.
3. Maker's mark.

1544 1. Leopard's Head, crowned. 2. Date Letter.
3. Maker's mark. 4. Lion Passant.

1697 1. Britannia. 2. Lion's Head erased. 3. Date
letter. 4. Maker's mark.

1719 1. Leopard's Head crowned. 2. Lion Passant.
3. Date Letter. 4. Maker's mark.

1784 1. Leopard's Head, crowned. 2. Lion Passant.
3. Date letter. 4. Maker's mark. 5. Sovereign's head.

1821 1. Leopard's Head, uncrowned. 2. Lion Passant. 3. Date letter. 4. Maker's mark. 5.
Sovereign's head.

1890 1. Leopard's Head. 2. Lion Passant. 3. Date
letter. 4. Maker's mark.

From 1844, Crown and 22 was used for gold instead
of Lion Passant.

		𝕬	1498–9
𝕭	1479–80	𝕭	1499–00
		𝕮	1500–1
𝕯	1481–2	𝕯	1501–2
		𝕰	1503–4
𝕳	1485–6	𝕲	1504–5
		𝕴	1506–7
		𝕶	1507–8
𝖀	1488–9	𝕷	1508–9
		𝕸	1509–10
𝕹	1490–1	𝕹	1510–1
𝕺	1491–2	𝕺	1511–2
		𝕻	1512–3
𝕼	1493–4	𝕼	1513–4
𝕽	1494–5	𝕿	1514–5
		𝖘	1515–6
𝕿	1496–7	𝕥	1516–7
		𝖛	1517–8

1518–9	1538–9	1558–9	1578–9
1519–20	1539–40	1559–60	1579–80
1520–1	1540–1	1560–1	1580–1
1521–2	1541–2	1561–2	1581–2
1522–3		1562–3	1582–3
1523–4	1543–4	1563–4	1583–4
1524–5		1564–5	1584–5
1525–6	1545–6	1565–6	1585–6
	1546–7	1566–7	1586–7
1527–8	1547–8	1567–8	1587–8
1528–9	1548–9	1568–9	1588–9
1529–30	1549–50	1569–70	1589–90
1530–1	1550–1	1570–1	1590–1
1531–2	1551–2	1571–2	1591–2
1532–3	1552–3	1572–3	1592–3
1533–4	1553–4	1573–4	1593–4
1534–5	1554–5	1574–5	1594–5
1535–6	1555–6	1575–6	1595–6
1536–7	1556–7	1576–7	1596–7
1537–8	1557–8	1577–8	1597–8

	1598–9		1618–9		1638–9		1658–9
	1599–00		1619–20		1639–40		1659–60
	1600–1		1620–1		1640–1		1660–1
	1601–2		1621–2		1641–2		1661–2
	1602–3		1622–3		1642–3		1662–3
	1603–4		1623–4		1643–4		1663–4
	1604–5		1624–5		1644–5		1664–5
	1605–6		1625–6		1645–6		1665–6
	1606–7		1626–7		1646–7		1666–7
	1607–8		1627–8		1647–8		1667–8
	1608–9		1628–9		1648–9		1668–9
	1609–10		1629–30		1649–50		1669–70
	1610–1		1630–1		1650–1		1670–1
	1611–2		1631–2		1651–2		1671–2
	1612–3		1632–3		1652–3		1672–3
	1613–4		1633–4		1653–4		1673–4
	1614–5		1634–5		1654–5		1674–5
	1615–6		1635–6		1655–6		1675–6
	1616–7		1636–7		1656–7		1676–7
	1617–8		1637–8		1657–8		1677–8

a	1678–9	A	1697	A	1716–7	a	1736–7
b	1679–80	B	1697–8	B	1717–8	b	1737–8
c	1680–1	C	1698–9	C	1718–9	c	1738–9
d	1681–2	D	1699–00	D	1719–20	d	1739–40
e	1682–3	E	1700–1	E	1720–1	e	1740–1
f	1683–4	F	1701–2	F	1721–2	f	1741–2
g	1684–5	G	1702–3	G	1722–3	g	1742–3
h	1685–6	H	1703–4	H	1723–4	h	1743–4
i	1686–7	I	1704–5	I	1724–5	i	1744–5
k	1687–8	K	1705–6	K	1725–6	k	1745–6
l	1688–9	L	1706–7	L	1726–7	l	1746–7
m	1689–90	M	1707–8	M	1727–8	m	1747–8
n	1690–1	N	1708–9	N	1728–9	n	1748–9
o	1691–2	O	1709–10	O	1729–30	o	1749–50
p	1692–3	P	1710–1	P	1730–1	p	1750–1
q	1693–4	Q	1711–2	Q	1731–2	q	1751–2
r	1694–5	R	1712–3	R	1732–3	r	1752–3
s	1695–6	S	1713–4	S	1733–4	f	1753–4
t	1696–7	T	1714–5	T	1734–5	t	1754–5
		U	1715–6	V	1735–6	u	1755–6

𝕬	1756–7	𝖆	1776–7	A	1796–7	𝖆	1816–7
𝕭	1757–8	𝖇	1777–8	B	1797–8	𝖇	1817–8
𝕮	1758–9	𝖈	1778–9	C	1798–9	𝖈	1818–9
𝕯	1759–60	𝖉	1779–80	D	1799–00	𝖉	1819–20
𝕰	1760–1	𝖊	1780–1	E	1800–1	𝖊	1820–1
𝕱	1761–2	𝖋	1781–2	F	1801–2	𝖋	1821–2
𝕲	1762–3	𝖌	1782–3	G	1802–3	𝖌	1822–3
𝕳	1763–4	𝖍	1783–4	H	1803–4	𝖍	1823–4
𝕴	1764–5	𝖎	1784–5	I	1804–5	𝖎	1824–5
𝕶	1765–6	𝖐	1785–6	K	1805–6	𝖐	1825–6
𝕷	1766–7	𝖑	1786–7	L	1806–7	𝖑	1826–7
𝕸	1767–8	𝖒	1787–8	M	1807–8	𝖒	1827–8
𝕹	1768–9	𝖓	1788–9	N	1808–9	𝖓	1828–9
𝕺	1769–70	𝖔	1789–90	O	1809–10	𝖔	1829–30
𝕻	1770–1	𝖕	1790–1	P	1810–1	𝖕	1830–1
𝕼	1771–2	𝖖	1791–2	Q	1811–2	𝖖	1831–2
𝕽	1772–3	𝖗	1792–3	R	1812–3	𝖗	1832–3
𝕾	1773–4	𝖘	1793–4	S	1813–4	𝖘	1833–4
𝕿	1774–5	𝖙	1794–5	U	1814–5	𝖙	1834–5
𝖀	1775–6	𝖚	1795–6	U	1815–6	𝖚	1835–6

𝕬	1836–7	𝖆	1856–7	A	1876–7	a	1896–7
𝕭	1837–8	𝖇	1857–8	B	1877–8	b	1897–8
𝕮	1838–9	𝖈	1858–9	C	1878–9	c	1898–9
𝕯	1839–40	𝖉	1859–60	D	1879–80	d	1899–00
𝕰	1840–1	𝖊	1860–1	E	1880–1	e	1900–1
𝕱	1841–2	𝖋	1861–2	F	1881–2	f	1901–2
𝕲	1842–3	𝖌	1862–3	G	1882–3	g	1902–3
𝕳	1843–4	𝖍	1863–4	H	1883–4	h	1903–4
𝕵	1844–5	𝖎	1864–5	I	1884–5	i	1904–5
𝕶	1845–6	𝖐	1865–6	K	1885–6	k	1905–6
𝕷	1846–7	𝖑	1866–7	L	1886–7	l	1906–7
𝕸	1847–8	𝖒	1867–8	M	1887–8	m	1907–8
𝕹	1848–9	𝖓	1868–9	N	1888–9	n	1908–9
𝕺	1849–50	𝖔	1869–70	O	1889–90	o	1909–10
𝕻	1850–1	𝖕	1870–1	P	1890–1	p	1910–1
𝕼	1851–2	𝖖	1871–2	Q	1891–2	q	1911–2
𝕽	1852–3	𝖗	1872–3	R	1892–3	r	1912–3
𝕾	1853–4	𝖘	1873–4	S	1893–4	s	1913–4
𝕿	1854–5	𝖙	1874–5	T	1894–5	t	1914–5
𝖀	1855–6	𝖚	1875–6	U	1895–6	u	1915–6

(a)	1916–7	(A)	1936–7	(a)	1956–7
(b)	1917–8	(B)	1937–8	(b)	1957–8
(c)	1918–9	(C)	1938–9	(C)	1958–9
(d)	1919–20	(D)	1939–40	(d)	1959–60
(e)	1920–1	(E)	1940–1	(e)	1960–1
(f)	1921–2	(F)	1941–2	(f)	1961–2
(g)	1922–3	(G)	1942–3	(g)	1962–3
(h)	1923–4	(H)	1943–4	(h)	1963–4
(i)	1924–5	(I)	1944–5	(i)	1964–5
(k)	1925–6	(K)	1945–6	(k)	1965–6
(l)	1926–7	(L)	1946–7	(l)	1966–7
(m)	1927–8	(M)	1947–8	(m)	1967–8
(n)	1928–9	(N)	1948–9	(n)	1968–9
(o)	1929–30	(O)	1949–50		
(p)	1930–1	(P)	1950–1		
(q)	1931–2	(Q)	1951–2		
(r)	1932–3	(R)	1952–3		
(s)	1933–4	(S)	1953–4		
(t)	1934–5	(T)	1954–5		
(u)	1935–6	(U)	1955–6		

BIRMINGHAM

From
1773 1. Anchor. 2. Lion Passant. 3. Date letter. 4. Maker's initials.

1784 1. Anchor. 2. Lion Passant. 3. Date letter. 4. Maker's initials. 5. Sovereign's head.

1890 1. Anchor. 2. Lion Passant. 3. Date letter. 4. Maker's initials.

A	1773–4
B	1774–5
C	1775–6
D	1776–7
E	1777–8
F	1778–9
G	1779–80
H	1780–1
I	1781–2
K	1782–3
L	1783–4
M	1784–5
N	1785–6
O	1786–7
P	1787–8
Q	1788–9
R	1789–90
S	1790–1
T	1791–2
U	1792–3
V	1793–4
W	1794–5
X	1795–6
Y	1796–7
Z	1797–8

a	1798–9	Ⓐ	1824–5	A	1849–50	𝕒	1875–6
b	1799–00	B	1825–6	B	1850–1	ⓑ	1876–7
c	1800–1	C	1826–7	C	1851–2	c	1877–8
d	1801–2	D	1827–8	D	1852–3	d	1878–9
e	1802–3	G	1828–9	E	1853–4	e	1879–80
f	1803–4	F	1829–30	F	1854–5	f	1880–1
g	1804–5			G	1855–6	g	1881–2
h	1805–6	Ⓖ	1830–1	H	1856–7	h	1882–3
ⓘ	1806–7	H	1831–2	I	1857–8	i	1883–4
			1832–3			k	1884–5
j	1807–8	K	1833–4	J	1858–9	l	1885–6
k	1808–9	L	1834–5	K	1859–60		
l	1809–10	M	1835–6	L	1860–1	m	1886–7
m	1810–1	N	1836–7	M	1861–2	n	1887–8
n	1811–2	O	1837–8	N	1862–3	o	1888–9
o	1812–3	P	1838–9	O	1863–4	p	1889–90
p	1813–4	Q	1839–40	P	1864–5	q	1890–1
q	1814–5	Ⓡ	1840–1	Q	1865–6	r	1891–2
r	1815–6		1841–2	R	1866–7	s	1892–3
s	1816–7	T	1842–3	Ⓢ	1867–8	t	1893–4
t	1817–8	U	1843–4	T	1868–9	u	1894–5
u	1818–9	V	1844–5	U	1869–70	v	1895–6
v	1819–20	W	1845–6	V	1870–1	w	1896–7
w	1820–1	X	1846–7	W	1871–2	x	1897–8
x	1821–2	Y	1847–8	X	1872–3	y	1898–9
y	1822–3	Z	1848–9	Y	1873–4	ʒ	1899–00
z	1823–4			Z	1874–5		

a	1900–1	A	1925–6	A	1950–1
b	1901–2	B	1926–7	B	1951–2
c	1902–3	C	1927–8	C	1952–3
d	1903–4	D	1928–9	D	1953–4
e	1904–5	E	1929–30	E	1954–5
f	1905–6	F	1930–1	F	1955–6
g	1906–7	G	1931–2	G	1956–7
h	1907–8	H	1932–3	H	1957–8
i	1908–9	J	1933–4	J	1958–9
k	1909–10	K	1934–5	K	1959–60
l	1910–1	L	1935–6	L	1960–1
m	1911–2	M	1936–7	M	1961–2
n	1912–3	N	1937–8	N	1962–3
o	1913–4	O	1938–9	O	1963–4
p	1914–5	P	1939–40	P	1964–5
q	1915–6	Q	1940–1	Q	1965–6
r	1916–7	R	1941–2	R	1966–7
s	1917–8	S	1942–3	S	1967–8
t	1919–9	T	1943–4	T	1968–9
u	1919–20	U	1944–5		
v	1920–1	V	1945–6		
w	1921–2	W	1946–7		
X	1922–3	X	1947–8		
y	1923–4	Y	1948–9		
Z	1924–5	Z	1949–50		

CHESTER

From
1701 1. City Arms, 3 demi-lions and 3 half gerbes (= wheatsheaves). 2. Britannia. 3. Lion's Head, erased. 4. Date letter. 5. Maker's mark.

1719 1. City Arms. 2. Lion Passant. 3. Leopard's Head, crowned. 4. Date letter. 5. Maker's mark.

1779 1. City Arms, sword between 3 gerbes. 2. Lion Passant. 3. Leopard's Head, crowned. 4. Date letter. 5. Maker's mark.

1784 1. City Arms. 2. Lion Passant. 3. Leopard's Head, crowned. 4. Date letter. 5. Maker's mark. 6. Sovereign's Head.

1823 1. City Arms. 2. Lion Passant. 3. Leopard's Head, uncrowned. 4. Date letter. 5. Maker's mark. 6. Sovereign's Head.

1839 1. City Arms. 2. Lion Passant. 3. Date letter. 4. Maker's mark. 5. Sovereign's Head.

1890 1. City Arms. 2. Lion Passant. 3. Date letter. 4. Maker's mark.

 1687–9

 1689–92

1692–3

A	1701–2	A	1726–7	a	1751–2	a	1776–7
B	1702–3	B	1727–8	b	1752–3	b	1777–8
C	1703–4	C	1728–9	c	1753–4	c	1778–9
D	1704–5	D	1729–30	d	1754–5	d	1779–80
E	1705–6	E	1730–1	e	1755–6	e	1780–1
F	1706–7	F	1731–2	f	1756–7	f	1781–2
G	1707–8	G	1732–3	G	1757–8	g	1782–3
H	1708–9	H	1733–4	h	1758–9	h	1783–4
I	1709–10	I	1734–5	i	1759–60	i	1784–5
K	1710–1	K	1735–6	k	1760–1	k	1785–6
L	1711–2	L	1736–7	l	1761–2	l	1786–7
M	1712–3	M	1737–8	m	1762–3	m	1787–8
N	1713–4	N	1738–9	n	1763–4	n	1788–9
O	1714–5	O	1739–40	o	1764–5	o	1789–90
P	1715–6	P	1740–1	P	1765–6	p	1790–1
Q	1716–7	Q	1741–2	Q	1766–7	q	1791–2
R	1717–8	R	1742–3	R	1767–8	r	1792–3
S	1718–9	S	1743–4	S	1768–9	s	1793–4
T	1719–20	T	1744–5	T	1769–70	t	1794–5
U	1720–1	U	1745–6	T	1770–1		
V	1721–2	V	1746–7	U	1771–2	u	1795–6
W	1722–3	W	1747–8	V	1772–3	v	1796–7
X	1723–4	X	1748–9	W	1773–4		
Y	1724–5	Y	1749–50	X	1774–5		
Z	1725–6	Z	1750–1	Y	1775–6		

A 1797–8	A 1818–9	𝕬 1839–40	𝖆 1864–5
B 1798–9	B 1819–20	𝕭 1840–1	𝖇 1865–6
C 1799–00	C 1820–1	𝕮 1841–2	𝖈 1866–7
D 1800–1	D 1821–2	𝕯 1842–3	𝖉 1867–8
E 1801–2	E 1822–3	𝕰 1843–4	𝖊 1868–9
F 1802–3	F 1823–4	𝕱 1844–5	𝖋 1869–70
G 1803–4	G 1824–5	𝕲 1845–6	𝖌 1870–1
H 1804–5	H 1825–6	𝕳 1846–7	𝖍 1871–2
I 1805–6	I 1826–7	𝕴 1847–8	𝖎 1872–3
K 1806–7	K 1827–8	𝕶 1848–9	𝖐 1873–4
L 1807–8	L 1828–9	𝕷 1849–50	𝖑 1874–5
M 1808–9	M 1829–30	𝕸 1850–1	𝖒 1875–6
N 1809–10	N 1830–1	𝕹 1851–2	𝖓 1876–7
O 1810–1	O 1831–2	𝕺 1852–3	𝖔 1877–8
P 1811–2	P 1832–3	𝕻 1853–4	𝖕 1878–9
Q 1812–3	Q 1833–4	𝕼 1854–5	𝖖 1879–80
R 1813–4	R 1834–5	𝕽 1855–6	𝖗 1880–1
S 1814–5	S 1835–6	𝕾 1856–7	𝖘 1881–2
T 1815–6	T 1836–7	𝕿 1857–8	𝖙 1882–3
U 1816–7	U 1837–8	𝖀 1858–9	𝖚 1883–4
V 1817–8	V 1838–9	𝖁 1859–60	
		𝖂 1860–1	
		𝖃 1861–2	
		𝖄 1862–3	
		𝖅 1863–4	

A	1884–5	A	1901–2	I	1926–7	A	1951–2
B	1885–6	B	1902–3	B	1927–8	B	1952–3
C	1886–7	C	1903–4	C	1928–9	C	1953–4
D	1887–8	D	1904–5	D	1929–30	D	1954–5
E	1888–9	E	1905–6	E	1930–1	E	1955–6
F	1889–90	F	1906–7	ff	1931–2	F	1956–7
G	1890–1	G	1907–8	G	1932–3	G	1957–8
H	1891–2	H	1908–9	H	1933–4	H	1958–9
I	1892–3	J	1909–10	J	1934–5	J	1959–60
K	1893–4	K	1910–1	K	1935–6	K	1960–1
L	1894–5	L	1911–2	L	1936–7	L	1961–2
M	1895–6	M	1912–3	M	1937–8	M	1962–3
N	1896–7	N	1913–4	N	1938–9		
O	1897–8	O	1914–5	O	1939–40		
P	1898–9	P	1915–6	P	1940–1		
Q	1899–00	Q	1916–7	Q	1941–2		
R	1900–1	R	1917–8	R	1942–3		
		S	1918–9	S	1943–4		
		T	1919–20	Z	1944–5		
		U	1920–1	U	1945–6		
		V	1921–2	V	1946–7		
		W	1922–3	W	1947–8		
		X	1923–4	X	1948–9		
		Y	1924–5	Y	1949–50		
		Z	1925–6	Z	1950–1		

EXETER

From

1701   1. Castle. 2. Lion's Head,
       erased.   3. Britannia.
       4. Date letter. 5. Maker's
       initials.

1721   1. Castle. 2. Lion Passant.
       3. Leopard's Head, crown-
       ed.   4. Date letter.
       5. Maker's initials.

1777   1. Castle. 2. Lion Passant.
       3. Date letter. 4. Maker's
       initials.

1784   1. Castle. 2. Lion Passant.
       3. Date letter. 4. Maker's
       initials.   5. Sovereign's
       Head.

A	1701–2
B	1702–3
C	1703–4
D	1704–5
E	1705–6
F	1706–7
G	1707–8
H	1708–9
I	1709–10
K	1710–1
L	1711–2
M	1712–3
N	1713–4
O	1714–5
P	1715–6
Q	1716–7
R	1717–8
S	1718–9
T	1719–20
V	1720–1
W	1721–2
X	1722–3
Y	1723–4
Z	1724–5

a	1725–6	A	1749–50	A	1773–4	A	1797–8
b	1726–7	B	1750–1	B	1774–5	B	1798–9
c	1727–8	C	1751–2	C	1775–6	C	1799–00
d	1728–9	D	1752–3	D	1776–7	D	1800–1
e	1729–30	E	1753–4	E	1777–8	E	1801–2
f	1730–1	F	1754–5	F	1778–9	F	1802–3
g	1731–2	G	1755–6	G	1779–80	G	1803–4
h	1732–3	H	1756–7	H	1780–1	H	1804–5
i	1733–4	I	1757–8	I	1781–3	I	1805–6
k	1734–5	K	1758–9	K	1783–4	K	1806–7
l	1735–6	L	1759–60	L	1784–5	L	1807–8
m	1736–7	M	1760–1	M	1785–6	M	1808–9
n	1737–8	N	1761–2	N	1786–7	N	1809–10
o	1738–9	O	1762–3	O	1787–8	O	1810–1
p	1739–40	P	1763–4	P	1788–9	P	1811–2
q	1740–1	Q	1764–5	q	1789–90	Q	1812–3
r	1741–2	R	1765–6	r	1790–1	R	1813–4
s	1742–3	S	1766–7	f	1791–2	S	1814–5
t	1743–4	T	1767–8	t	1792–3	T	1815–6
u	1744–5	V	1768–9	u	1793–4	U	1816–7
w	1745–6	W	1769–70	w	1794–5		
x	1746–7	X	1770–1	x	1795–6		
y	1747–8	Y	1771–2	y	1796–7		
z	1748–9	Z	1772–3				

ⓐ	1817–8	Ⓐ	1837–8	Ⓐ	1857–8	Ⓐ 1877–8
b	1818–9	ℬ	1838–9	B	1858–9	Ⓑ 1878–9
c	1819–20	ℭ	1839–40	C	1859–60	Ⓒ 1879–80
d	1820–1	𝕯	1840–1	D	1860–1	Ⓓ 1880–1
e	1821–2	𝕰	1841–2	E	1861–2	Ⓔ 1881–2
f	1822–3	𝕱	1842–3	F	1862–3	Ⓕ 1882–3
g	1823–4	𝕲	1843–4	G	1863–4	
h	1824–5	𝕳	1844–5	H	1864–5	
i	1825–6	𝕴	1845–6	I	1865–6	
k	1826–7	𝕶	1846–7	K	1866–7	
l	1827–8	𝕷	1847–8	L	1867–8	
m	1828–9	Ⓜ	1848–9	M	1868–9	
n	1829–30	𝕹	1849–50	N	1869–70	
o	1830–1	𝕺	1850–1	O	1870–1	
p	1831–2	𝕻	1851–2	P	1871–2	
q	1832–3	𝕼	1852–3	Q	1872–3	
r	1833–4	𝕽	1853–4	R	1873–4	
s	1834–5	Ⓢ	1854–5	S	1874–5	
t	1835–6	𝕿	1855–6	T	1875–6	
u	1836–7	𝖀	1856–7	U	1876–7	

NEWCASTLE

From
1702   1. Three Castles.   2. Lion's Head, erased.
3. Britannia.   4. Date letter.   5. Maker's
initials.

1721   1. Three Castles.   2. Lion Passant.   3. Leopard's Head, crowned.   4. Date letter.   5.
Maker's initials.

1784   1. Three Castles.   2. Lion Passant.   3. Leopard's Head, crowned.   4. Date letter.   5.
Maker's initials.   6. Sovereign's Head.

1846   1. Three Castles.   2. Lion Passant.   3. Leopard's Head, uncrowned.   4. Date letter.   5.
Maker's initials.   6. Sovereign's Head.

Letter S of 1784-5 is found both with and without
the sovereign's head.

𝕬	1702–3	ⓐ	1721–2	A	1740–1	𝓡	1759–60
𝕭	1703–4	𝔅	1722–3	B	1741–2	𝓑	1760–1
		ℭ	1723–4	C	1742–3	𝓒	1769–70
𝕯	1705–6	𝔇	1724–5	D	1743–4	𝓓	770–1
				E	1744–5		
𝕱	1707–8			F	1745–6	𝓙	1772–3
		𝔊	1727–8	G	1746–7	G	1773–4
		𝔥	1728–9	H	1747–8	H	1774–5
		𝔍	1729–30	I	1748–9		
				K	1749–50	K	1776–7
𝕸	1712–3			L	1750–1		
		𝔐	1732–3	M	1751–2	N	1779–80
				N	1752–3	O	1780–1
		𝔒	1734–5	O	1753–4	P	1781–2
				P	1754–5	Q	1782–3
𝕺	1716–7	𝔔	1736–7	Q	1755–6	R	1783–4
						S	1784–5
𝕼	1718–9	ℜ	1737–8	R	1756–7	T	1785–6
𝕯	1719–20	𝔖	1738–9	S	1757–8	U	1786–7
				T	1758–9	X	1788–9
						Y	1789–90
						Z	1790–1

A	1791–2	A	1815–6	A	1839–40	a	1864–5
B	1792–3	B	1816–7	B	1840–1	b	1865–6
		C	1817–8	C	1841–2		
D	1794–5	D	1818–9	D	1842–3	c	1866–7
E	1795–6	E	1819–20	E	1843–4	d	1867–8
		F	1820–1	F	1844–5	e	1868–9
G	1797–8	G	1821–2	G	1845–6	f	1869–70
H	1798–9	H	1822–3	H	1846–7	g	1870–1
I	1799–00	I	1823–4	I	1847–8	h	1871–2
K	1800–1	K	1824–5	J	1848–9	i	1872–3
L	1801–2	L	1825–6	K	1849–50	k	1873–4
M	1802–3	M	1826–7	L	1850–1	l	1874–5
N	1803–4	N	1827–8	M	1851–2	m	1875–6
O	1804–5	O	1828–9	N	1852–3	n	1876–7
P	1805–6	P	1829–30	O	1853–4	o	1877–8
Q	1806–7	Q	1830–1	P	1854–5	p	1878–9
R	1807–8	R	1831–2	Q	1855–6	q	1879–80
S	1808–9	S	1832–3	R	1856–7	r	1880–1
T	1809–10	T	1833–4	S	1857–8	s	1881–2
U	1810–1	V	1834–5	T	1858–9	t	1882–3
W	1811–2	W	1835–6	U	1859–60	u	1883–4
X	1812–3	X	1836–7	W	1860–1		
Y	1813–4	Y	1837–8	X	1861–2		
Z	1814–5	Z	1838–9	Y	1862–3		
				Z	1863–4		

A	1565–6	A	1624–5	a	1688–9
B	1566–7	B	1625–6	b	1689–90
C	1567–8	C	1626–7		
D	1568–9	D	1627–8	d	1691–2
E	1569–70	E	1628–9	I	1696–7
F	1570–1			K	1697–8
G	1571–2	G	1630–1	A	1701–2
I	1573–4	I	1632–3		
K	1574–5	K	1633–4		
R	1581	L	1634–5		
		M	1635–6		
		N	1636–7		
		O	1637–8		
		P	1638–9		
		Q	1639–40		
		R	1640–1		
		S	1641–2		
		T	1642–3		

NORWICH

Castle over Lion,
and occasionally
Tudor Rose crowned.

SHEFFIELD

From
1773   1 Crown. 2. Lion Passant.
       3. Date letter. 4. Maker's
       mark.
1784   1. Crown. 2. Lion Passant.
       3. Date letter. 4. Maker's
       mark. 5. Sovereign's Head.
1890   1. Crown. 2. Lion Passant.
       3. Date letter. 4. Maker's
       mark.

Crown and date letter contained
in one stamp on small objects
1780–1853.

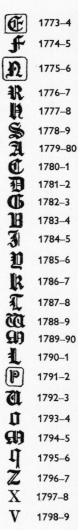

𝕰	1773–4
𝖋	1774–5
𝕹	1775–6
𝕽	1776–7
𝕳	1777–8
𝕾	1778–9
𝕬	1779–80
𝕮	1780–1
𝕯	1781–2
𝕲	1782–3
𝕳	1783–4
𝕴	1784–5
𝕻	1785–6
𝕶	1786–7
𝕿	1787–8
𝕸	1788–9
𝕸	1789–90
𝕷	1790–1
𝕻	1791–2
𝖀	1792–3
𝕺	1793–4
𝕸	1794–5
𝖖	1795–6
𝖅	1796–7
X	1797–8
V	1798–9

Letter	Year	Letter	Year	Letter	Year	Letter	Year
(crowned) E	1799–100	(crown) a	1824–5	A (crown)	1844–5	A	1868–9
N	1800–1	b	1825–6	B	1845–6	B	1869–70
H	1801–2	c	1826–7	C	1846–7	C	1870–1
M	1802–3	(crown) d	1827–8	D	1847–8	D	1871–2
F	1803–4	e	1828–9	E	1848–9	E	1872–3
G	1804–5	f	1829–30	F	1849–50	F	1873–4
B	1805–6	g	1830–1	G	1850–1	G	1874–5
A	1806–7	(crown) h	1831–2	H	1851–2	H	1875–6
S	1807–8	k	1832–3	I	1852–3	J	1876–7
P	1808–9	l	1833–4	K	1853–4	K	1877–8
K	1809–10	m	1834–5	L	1854–5	L	1878–9
L	1810–1	p	1835–6	M	1855–6	M	1879–80
C	1811–2	q	1836–7	N	1856–7	N	1880–1
D	1812–3	r	1837–8	O	1857–8	O	1881–2
R	1813–4	s	1838–9	P	1858–9	P	1882–3
W	1814–5	t	1839–40	R	1859–60	Q	1883–4
O	1815–6	u	1840–1	S	1860–1	R	1884–5
T	1816–7	v	1841–2	T	1861–2	S	1885–6
X	1817–8	x	1842–3	U	1862–3	T	1886–7
I	1818–9	z	1843–4	V	1863–4	U	1887–8
V	1819–20			W	1864–5	V	1888–9
Q	1820–1			X	1865–6	W	1889–90
Y	1821–2			Y	1866–7	X	1890–1
Z	1822–3			Z	1867–8	Y	1891–2
U	1823–4					Z	1892–3

𝔞	1893–4	ⓐ	1918–9	𝐀	1943–4	𝒜 1968–9
𝔟	1894–5	ⓑ	1919–20	𝐁	1944–5	
𝔠	1895–6	ⓒ	1920–1	𝐂	1945–6	
𝔡	1896–7	ⓓ	1921–2	𝐃	1946–7	
𝔢	1897–8	ⓔ	1922–3	𝐄	1947–8	
𝔣	1898–9	ⓕ	1923–4	𝐅	1948–9	
𝔤	1899–00	ⓖ	1924–5	𝐆	1949–50	
𝔥	1900–1	ⓗ	1925–6	𝐇	1950–1	
𝔦	1901–2	ⓘ	1926–7	𝐈	1951–2	
𝔨	1902–3	ⓚ	1927–8	𝐊	1952–3	
𝔩	1903–4	ⓛ	1928–9	𝐋	1953–4	
𝔪	1904–5	ⓜ	1929–30	𝐌	1954–5	
𝔫	1905–6	ⓝ	1930–1	𝐍	1955–6	
𝔬	1906–7	ⓞ	1931–2	𝐎	1956–7	
𝔭	1907–8	ⓟ	1932–3	𝐏	1957–8	
𝔮	1908–9	ⓠ	1933–4	𝐐	1958–9	
𝔯	1909–10	ⓡ	1934–5	𝐑	1959–60	
𝔰	1910–1	ⓢ	1935–6	𝐒	1960–1	
𝔱	1911–2	ⓣ	1936–7	𝐓	1961–2	
𝔲	1912–3	ⓤ	1937–8	𝐔	1962–3	
𝔳	1913–4	ⓥ	1938–9	𝐕	1963–4	
𝔴	1914–5	ⓦ	1939–40	𝐖	1964–5	
𝔵	1915–6	ⓧ	1940–1	𝐗	1965–6	
𝔶	1916–7	ⓨ	1941–2	𝐘	1966–7	
𝔷	1917–8	ⓩ	1942–3	𝐙	1967–8	

YORK

From

1562   1. Half Fleur de Lys and half Leopard's Head. 2. Date letter. 3. Maker's mark.

1632   1. Half Fleurs de Lys and half Rose, crowned. 2. Date letter. 3. Maker's mark.

1700   1. Five Lions on a Cross. 2. Britannia. 3. Lion's Head, erased. 4. Date letter. 5. Maker's mark.

1779   1. Five Lions on a Cross. 2. Lion Passant. 3. Leopard's Head, crowned. 4. Date letter. 5. Maker's mark.

1784   1. Five Lions on a Cross. 2. Lion Passant. 3. Leopard's Head, crowned. 4. Sovereign's Head. 5. Date letter. 6. Maker's mark.

1848   1. Five Lions on a Cross. 2. Lion Passant. 3. Sovereign's Head. 4. Date letter. 5. Maker's mark.

		𝔅	1608–9
		𝔠	1609–10
		𝔇	1610–1
		𝔈	1611–2
		𝔉	1612–3
		𝔊	1613–4
		𝔥	1614–5
		𝔍	1615–6
𝕶 1568-9		𝔨	1616–7
𝕷 1569–70			
	𝔨 1592–3		
		𝔐	1618–9
		𝔑	1619–20
𝕼 1574–5		𝔓	1621–2
		𝔐	1622–3
𝐑 1575–6		𝔓	1623–4
		𝔖	1624–5
𝐓 1577–8	𝔑 1599–00	𝔗	1625–6
		𝔘	1626–7
		𝔚	1627–8
𝐙 1582–3		𝔓	1629–30
		𝐙	1630–1

𝔟 1584–5

a	1631–2	*A*	1657–8	**A**	1682–3
b	1632–3			**B**	1683–4
c	1633–4			**C**	1684–5
d	1634–5	*D*	1660–1	**D**	1685–6
e	1635–6	*E*	1661–2	**e**	1686–7
f	1636–7	*F*	1662–3	**F**	1687–8
g	1637–8	*G*	1663–4	**G**	1688–9
h	1638–9	*H*	1664–5	**h**	1689–90
k	1641–2			**K**	1691–2
l	1642–3	*K*	1666–7		
		M	1668–9	**M**	1693–4
		P	1671–2		
		Q	1672–3	**O**	1695–6
		R	1673–4	**P**	1696–7
t	1650–1	*S*	1674–5	**Q**	1697–8
		T	1675–6		
		V	1677–8		
x	1654–5	*W*	1678–9		
y	1655–6	*X*	1679–80		
		Y	1680–1		
		Z	1681–2		

9

		ⓐ	1812–3	Ⓐ	1837–8
		b	1813–4	B	1838–9
		c	1814–5	C	1839–40
ⓓ	1790–1	d	1815–6	D	1840–1
ⓔ	1791–2	e	1816–7	E	1841–2
		f	1817–8	F	1842–3
ⓖ	1793–4	g	1818–9	G	1843–4
		h	1819–20	H	1844–5
ⓘ	1795–6	i	1820–1	I	1845–6
ⓚ	1796–7	k	1821–2	K	1846–7
		l	1822–3	L	1847–8
Ⓜ	1798–9	m	1823–4	M	1848–9
Ⓝ	1799–00	n	1824–5	N	1849–50
O	1800–1	o	1825–6	O	1850–1
P	1801–2	p	1826–7	P	1851–2
Ⓠ	1802–3	q	1827–8	Q	1852–3
R	1803–4	r	1828–9	R	1853–4
S	1804–5	s	1829–30	S	1854–5
T	1805–6	t	1830–1	T	1855–6
U	1806–7	u	1831–2	U	1856–7
V	1807–8	b	1832–3		
W	1808–9	w	1833–4		
X	1809–10	x	1834–5		
Ⓨ	1810–1	y	1835–6		
Z	1811–2	ȝ	1836–7		

EDINBURGH

From
1681   1. Castle.   2. Assay
Master's initials.   3. Date
letter.   4. Maker's mark.
1759   1. Castle.   2. Thistle.
3. Date letter.   4. Maker's
mark.
1784   1. Castle.   2. Thistle.
3. Date letter.   4. Maker's
mark.   5. Sovereign's head.
1890   1. Castle.   2. Thistle.
3. Date letter.   4. Maker's
mark.

𝖆	1681–2
𝖇	1682–3
𝖈	1683–4
𝖉	1684–5
𝖊	1685–6
𝖋	1686–7
𝖌	1687–8
𝖍	1688–9
𝖎	1689–90
𝖐	1690–1
𝖑	1691–2
𝖒	1692–3
𝖓	1693–4
𝖔	1694–5
𝖕	1695–6
𝖖	1696–7
𝖗	1697–8
𝖘	1698–9
𝖙	1699–00
𝖛	1700–1
𝖜	1701–2
𝖝	1702–3
𝖞	1703–4
𝖟	1704–5

A	1705–6	A	1730–1	A	1755–6	A	1780–1
B	1706–7	B	1731–2	B	1756–7	B	1781–2
C	1707–8	C	1732–3	C	1757–8	C	1782–3
D	1708–9	D	1733–4	D	1758–9	D	1783–4
E	1709–10	E	1734–5	E	1759–60	E	1784–5
F	1710–1	F	1735–6	F	1760–1	F	1785–6
G	1711–2	G	1736–7	G	1761–2	G	1786–7
H	1712–3	H	1737–8	H	1762–3	G	1787–8
I	1713–4	I	1738–9	I	1763–4	H	1788–9
K	1714–5	K	1739–40	K	1764–5	I	1789–90
L	1715–6	L	1740–1	L	1765–6	K	1790–1
M	1716–7	M	1741–2	M	1766–7	L	1791–2
N	1717–8	N	1742–3	N	1767–8	M	1792–3
O	1718–9	O	1743–4	O	1768–9	N	1793–4
P	1719–20	P	1744–5	P	1769–70	O	1794–5
Q	1720–1	Q	1745–6	Q	1770–1	P	1795–6
R	1721–2	R	1746–7	R	1771–2	Q	1796–7
S	1722–3	S	1747–8	S	1772–3	R	1797–8
T	1723–4	T	1748–9	T	1773–4	S	1798–9
U	1724–5	U	1749–50	U	1774–5	T	1799–00
V	1725–6	V	1750–1	V	1775–6	U	1800–1
W	1726–7	W	1751–2	X	1776–7	V	1801–2
X	1727–8	X	1752–3	Y	1777–8	W	1802–3
Y	1728–9	Y	1753–4	Z	1778–9	X	1803–4
Z	1729–30	Z	1754–5	U	1779–80	Y	1804–5
						Z	1805–6

a	1806–7	A	1832–3	A	1857–8	a	1882–3
b	1807–8	B	1833–4	B	1858–9	b	1883–4
c	1808–9	C	1834–5	C	1859–60	c	1884–5
d	1809–10	D	1835–6	D	1860–1	d	1885–6
e	1810–1	E	1836–7	E	1861–2	e	1886–7
f	1811–2	F	1837–8	F	1862–3	f	1887–8
g	1812–3	G	1838–9	G	1863–4	g	1888–9
h	1813–4	H	1839–40	H	1864–5	h	1889–90
i	1814–5	J	1840–1	I	1865–6	i	1890–1
j	1815–6	K	1841–2	K	1866–7	k	1891–2
k	1816–7	L	1842–3	L	1867–8	l	1892–3
l	1817–8	M	1843–4	M	1868–9	m	1893–4
m	1818–9	N	1844–5	N	1869–70	n	1894–5
n	1819–20	O	1845–6	O	1870–1	o	1895–6
o	1820–1	P	1846–7	P	1871–2	p	1896–7
p	1821–2	Q	1847–8	Q	1872–3	q	1897–8
q	1822–3	R	1848–9	R	1873–4	r	1898–9
r	1823–4	S	1849–50	S	1874–5	s	1899–00
s	1824–5	T	1850–1	T	1875–6	t	1900–1
t	1825–6	U	1851–2	U	1876–7	u	1901–2
u	1826–7	V	1852–3	V	1877–8	w	1902–3
v	1827–8	W	1853–4	W	1878–9	r	1903–4
w	1828–9	X	1854–5	X	1879–80	y	1904–5
x	1829–30	Y	1855–6	Y	1880–1	z	1905–6
y	1830–1	Z	1856–7	Z	1881–2		
z	1831–2						

Ⓐ	1906–7	𝒜	1931–2	𝕬	1956–7
Ⓑ	1907–8	ℬ	1932–3	𝕭	1957–8
Ⓒ	1908–9	𝒞	1933–4	𝕮	1958–9
Ⓓ	1909–10	𝒟	1934–5	𝕯	1959–60
Ⓔ	1910–1	ℰ	1935–6	𝕰	1960–1
Ⓕ	1911–2	ℱ	1936–7	𝖋	1961–2
Ⓖ	1912–3	𝒢	1937–8	𝕲	1962–3
Ⓗ	1913–4	𝒦	1938–9	𝕳	1963–4
Ⓘ	1914–5	𝒥	1939–40	𝕴	1964–5
Ⓚ	1915–6	𝒦	1940–1	𝕜	1965–6
Ⓛ	1916–7	ℒ	1941–2	𝕷	1966–7
Ⓜ	1917–8	ℳ	1942–3	𝕸	1967–8
Ⓝ	1918–9	𝒩	1943–4		
Ⓞ	1919–20	𝒪	1944–5		
Ⓟ	1920–1	𝒫	1945–6		
Ⓠ	1921–2	𝒬	1946–7		
Ⓡ	1922–3	ℛ	1947–8		
Ⓢ	1923–4	𝒮	1948–9		
Ⓣ	1924–5	𝒯	1949–50		
Ⓤ	1925–6	𝒰	1950–1		
Ⓥ	1926–7	𝒱	1951–2		
Ⓦ	1927–8	𝒲	1952–3		
Ⓧ	1928–9	𝒳	1953–4		
Ⓨ	1929–30	𝒴	1954–5		
Ⓩ	1930–1	𝒵	1955–6		

GLASGOW

From
1681   1. Tree, Fish and Bell. 2. Date letter. 3. Maker's mark (frequently duplicated).

1819   1. Tree, Fish and Bell. 2. Lion Rampant. 3. Date letter. 4. Maker's mark. 5. Sovereign's Head.

1890   1. Tree, Fish and Bell. 2. Lion Rampant. 3. Date letter. 4. Maker's mark.

1914   1. Tree, Fish and Bell. 2. Lion Rampant. 3. Thistle. 4. Date letter. 5. Maker's mark.

𝕼	1696–7	A	1819–20	𝔄	1845–6	A	1871–2
𝕾	1698–9	B	1820–1	𝔅	1846–7	B	1872–3
𝕿	1699–00	C	1821–2	ℭ	1847–8	C	1873–4
𝖀	1700–1	D	1822–3	𝔇	1848–9	D	1874–5
		E	1823–4	𝔈	1849–50	E	1875–6
𝖁	1701–2	F	1824–5	𝔉	1850–1	F	1876–7
		G	1825–6	𝔊	1851–2	G	1877–8
𝖂	1704–5	H	1826–7	𝔥	1852–3	H	1878–9
		I	1827–8	𝔧	1853–4	I	1879–80
𝖃	1705–6	J	1828–9	𝔧	1854–5	J	1880–1
Ⓑ	1707–8	K	1829–30	𝔨	1855–6	K	1881–2
		L	1830–1	𝔩	1856–7	L	1882–3
Ⓓ	1709–10	M	1831–2	𝔐	1857–8	M	1883–4
		N	1832–3	𝔑	1858–9	N	1884–5
		O	1833–4	𝔒	1859–60	O	1885–6
		P	1834–5	𝔓	1860–1	P	1886–7
		Q	1835–6	𝔔	1861–2	Q	1887–8
		R	1836–7	𝔯	1862–3	R	1888–9
		S	1837–8	𝔰	1863–4	S	1889–90
		T	1838–9	𝔗	1864–5	T	1890–1
		U	1839–40	𝔘	1865–6	U	1891–2
		V	1840–1	𝔙	1866–7	V	1892–3
		W	1841–2	𝔚	1867–8	W	1893–4
		X	1842–3	𝔵	1868–9	X	1894–5
		Y	1843–4	𝔜	1869–70	Y	1895–6
		Z	1844–5	𝔷	1870–1	Z	1896–7

A	1897–8	a	1923–4	A	1949–50
B	1898–9	b	1924–5	B	1950–1
C	1899–00	c	1925–6	C	1951–2
D	1900–1	d	1926–7	D	1952–3
E	1901–2	e	1927–8	e	1953–4
F	1902–3	f	1928–9	F	1954–5
G	1903–4	g	1929–30	3	1955–6
H	1904–5	h	1930–1	h	1956–7
J	1905–6	i	1931–2	l	1957–8
F	1906–7	j	1932–3	l	1958–9
K	1907–8	k	1933–4	m	1959–60
L	1908–9	I	1934–5	N	1960–1
M	1909–10	m	1935–6	O	1961–2
N	1910–1	n	1936–7	p	1962–3
O	1911–2	o	1937–8	R	1963–4
P	1912–3	p	1938–9		
Q	1913–4	q	1939–40		
R	1914–5	r	1940–1		
S	1915–6	s	1941–2		
T	1916–7	t	1942–3		
U	1917–8	u	1943–4		
V	1918–9	v	1944–5		
W	1919–20	w	1945–6		
X	1920–1	x	1946–7		
Y	1921–2	y	1947–8		
Z	1922–3	z	1948–9		

DUBLIN

From
1678 1. Harp crowned. 2. Date letter. 3. Maker's mark.

1731 1. Harp crowned. 2. Date letter. 3. Maker's mark. 4. Hibernia.

1784 1. Harp crowned (22 karat gold and silver), or Plume of Feathers (20 karat), or Unicorn (18 karat). 2. Date letter. 3. Maker's mark. 4. Hibernia.

1807 1. Harp crowned (22 karat gold and silver), or Plume of Feathers (20 karat), or Unicorn (18 karat). 2. Date letter. 3. Maker's mark. 4. Hibernia. 5. Sovereign's Head.

1890 1. Harp crowned (22 karat gold and silver), or Plume of Feathers (20 karat), or Unicorn (18 karat). 2. Date letter. 3. Maker's mark. 4. Hibernia.

A 1638–9   **B** 1659–60   **A** 1678–9   **A** 1717–8

B 1639–40   **f** 1663–4   **B** 1679–80   **B** 1718–9

C 1640–1   **g** 1664–5   **C** 1680–1

D 1641–2   **O** 1671–2   **D** 1681–2   **C** 1719–20

I 1646–7

S 1655–6   **G** 1685–7

T 1656–7

                                     k 1693–5

                                     L 1696–9

                                     M 1699–00

                                     N 1700–1

                                     O 1701–2

                                     P 1702–3

                                     R 1704–6

                                     S 1706–8

                                     T 1708–10

                                     U 1710–2

                                     X 1714–5

                                     Y 1715–6

𝕬	1720–1	Ⓐ	1747	Ⓐ	1773	Ⓐ	1797
B	1721–2	B	1748	B	1774	B	1798
C	1722–3	C	1749	C	1775	C	1799
D	1723–4	D	1750	D	1776	D	1800
E	1724–5	E	1751–2	E	1777	E	1801
F	1725–6	F	1752–3	F	1778	F	1802
G	1726–7	G	1753–4	G	1779	G	1803
H	1727–8	H	1754–5	H	1780	H	1804
I	1728–9	I	1757	I	1781	I	1805
K	1729–30	K	1758	K	1782	K	1806
L	1730–2	L	1759	L	1783	L	1807
M	1732–3	M	1760	M	1784	M	1808
N	1733–4	N	1761	N	1785	N	1809
O	1734–5	O	1762	O	1786	O	1810
P	1735–6	P	1763	P	1787	P	1811
Q	1736–7	Q	1764	Q	1788	Q	1812
R	1737–8	R	1765	R	1789	R	1813
S	1738–9	S	1766	S	1790	S	1814
T	1739–40	T	1767	T	1791	T	1815
U	1740–1	U	1768	U	1792	U	1816
W	1741–3	W	1769	W	1793	W	1817
X	1743–4	X	1770	X	1794	X	1818
Y	1745	Y	1771	Y	1795	Y	1819
Z	1746	Z	1772	Z	1796	Z	1820

Ⓐ	1821	ⓐ	1846–7	Ⓐ	1871–2	𝔄	1896–7
B	1822	ⓑ	1847–8	B	1872–3	𝔅	1897–8
C	1823	ⓒ	1848–9	C	1873–4	ℭ	1898–9
D	1824	ⓓ	1849–50	D	1874–5	𝔇	1899–00
Ⓔ ⓔ	1825–6	ⓔ	1850–1	E	1875–6	𝔈	1900–1
F	1826–7	f	1851–2	F	1876–7	𝔉	1901–2
G	1827–8	g	1852–3	G	1877–8	𝔊	1902–3
H	1828–9	h	1853–4	H	1878–9	𝔥	1903–4
I	1829–30	j	1854–5	I	1879–80	𝔍	1904–5
K	1830–1	ⓚ	1855–6	K	1880–1	𝔎	1905–6
L	1831–2	l	1856–7	L	1881–2	𝔏	1906–7
M	1832–3	m	1857–8	M	1882–3	𝔐	1907–8
N	1833–4	n	1858–9	N	1883–4	𝔑	1908–9
O	1834–5	o	1859–60	O	1884–5	𝔒	1909–10
P	1835–6	p	1860–1	P	1885–6	𝔓	1910–1
Q	1836–7	q	1861–2	Q	1886–7	𝔔	1911–2
R	1837–8	r	1862–3	R	1887–8	𝔎	1912–3
S	1838–9	s	1863–4	S	1888–9	𝔖	1913–4
T	1839–40	t	1864–5	T	1889–90	𝔗	1914–5
U	1840–1	u	1865–6	U	1890–1	𝔘	1915–6
V	1841–2	v	1866–7	V	1891–2		
W	1842–3	w	1867–8	W	1892–3		
X	1843–4	x	1868–9	X	1893–4		
Y	1844–5	y	1869–70	Y	1894–5		
Z	1845–6	z	1870–1	Z	1895–6		

Ⓐ	1916–7	A	1942	ⓐ	1968
ⓑ	1917–8	B	1943	ⓑ	1969
Ⓒ	1918–9	C	1944	ⓒ	1970
Ⓓ	1919–20	D	1945		
Ⓔ	1920–1	E	1946		
Ⓕ	1921–2	F	1947		
Ⓖ	1922–3	G	1948		
Ⓗ	1923–4	H	1949		
Ⓘ	1924–5	I	1950		
Ⓚ	1925–6	J	1951		
Ⓛ	1926–7	K	1952		
Ⓜ	1927–8	L	1953		
Ⓝ	1928–9	M	1954		
Ⓞ	1929–30	N	1955		
Ⓟ	1930–1	O	1956		
Ⓠ	1932	P	1957		
Ⓡ	1933	Q	1958		
Ⓢ	1934	R	1959		
Ⓣ	1935	S	1960		
Ⓤ	1936	T	1961		
Ⓥ	1937	U	1962		
Ⓦ	1938	V	1963		
Ⓧ	1939	W	1964		
Ⓨ	1940	X	1965		
Ⓩ	1941	Y	1966		
		Z	1967		

INDEX

CATALOGUE

OF

BOOKS

on

SILVERWARE

CERAMICS

etc.

Published

by

WILLIAM REEVES

Published

by

WILLIAM REEVES

Bookseller Ltd.

1a Norbury Crescent, London, S.W.16

List of prices supplied on application.

In addition to the books listed in this catalogue, we publish important books on music, and also freemasonry. These books are listed in special catalogues which will be sent on request.

Marks and Monograms on European & Oriental Pottery and Porcelain

By Wm. Chaffers

The British Section edited by G. A. Godden, F.R.S.A. The European and Oriental Sections edited by F. Litchfield & R. L. Hobson

2 Vols., 10 × 7 inches, 15th Revised Edition, over 1000 pages, 2 Plates in Colour, 12 Halftone Plates, 1965.

The Master work on Ceramics! Over 5,000 clearly reproduced identification marks, an exhaustive index and a thorough, scholarly survey of every historical period, manufacturing techniques and development.

A complete survey of marks and monograms of every historical period, designed for ease of reference. It is equally important as an extensive history of pottery and porcelain with an historical commentary on factories, potters, modellers and artists in every European and Oriental country contributing to the art of ceramics.

The book is introduced by three interesting chapters on Ancient Pottery, Romano-British Pottery and Mediaeval Earthenware Vessels. After this preface, the main body of the work on marks and monograms opens with an exhaustive study of Italian Majolica, followed by a similar study of French Fayence. There are considerable sections on the majolica and fayence of Spain, Portugal, Persia, Syria, Turkey, Russia, Scandinavia, Holland (especially Delft), Belgium and Germany.

Attention is then switched to the far East, where Chinese pottery and porcelain is described by R. L. Hobson in great detail, with reproductions of the reign marks, cyclical dates, numerals, marks of commendation, symbols etc. Japanese ceramics are also handled in a similar exhaustive fashion.

Returning to Europe the introduction of porcelain is traced, and the hard and soft paste types differentiated. Each country is then treated in detail commencing with Italy, especial attention being given to Florence, Doccia, Capo di Monte and Venice. Then follows a short but concise study of the factories of Spain and Portugal, and a detailed account of the Meissen wares. After this comes the history of the Vienna factory and the factories of Bohemia and the German states of

Prussia, Bavaria, Brunswick, Wurtemberg, Baden and Thuringia. There is a large section on France describing all the factories of any note, that of Sevres being given in very full detail. The European portion concludes with chapters on Switzerland, Holland and Belgium, Russia and Poland, and Scandinavia.

We then come to the large part of the book treating of British pottery and porcelain, and in this new revised edition there is much new material. Numerous past errors have been corrected and the Bow, Longton Hall and Lowestoft chapters have been completely re-written. Great care has been taken to date wherever possible the period of use of the marks illustrated. This has been made possible by detailed study of local directories and rate records. Much information on later marks has been supplied by the firms concerned, and in the case of former manufacturers, marks reproduced in trade journals have proved a rich source of documentary evidence both on the manufacturer's name and on the period of use of the mark.

Chaffers is of course much more than a mark book. It is a reference book giving detailed information on the histories of the various factories, the personalities involved, the types of ware produced, etc. It is the most quoted ceramic reference book in the world and this revised 15th edition marks a further step forward in presenting recent discoveries and research.

Collector's Handbook of Marks and Monograms on Pottery and Porcelain of the Renaissance and Modern Periods
By Wm. Chaffers

The authoritative, world-famous handbook containing over 5,000 marks and monograms, plus a ready reference index. The marks, signatures and monograms of factories of Fayence, Delft, Majolica, Pottery and Porcelain, with a large section on Chinese and Japanese are given, in many cases with the dates of time of existence, from thirteenth to twentieth century. It is a book for every collector, student, hobbyist and dealer.

Lord Chesterfield's Letters to his Son

Edited by C. S. Carey

2 Vols. 7½ × 5 ins. Pp. xii, 412, 426.

The Chesterfield Letters have enthralled and amused for nearly two centuries. The literary reputation of Chesterfield rests on the letters. Their shrewdness, wit and purity of style are universally admitted; their moral tone is more disputable, but modern criticism has tended to modify Johnson's severe strictures. The advice is always conveyed in a style which is a model of that urbanity which characterized the English nobility in the age preceding the regency.

This edition contains the full 395 Letters as well as a number of miscellaneous papers by the same hand. The letters in French have a full translation appended as have the numerous quotations in classical and modern tongues. The Notes are detailed and extraordinarily helpful. With Index, Biography of Lord Chesterfield, and extensive Notes.

The Haunted Homes and Family Traditions of Great Britain

By John H. Ingram

7½ × 5 ins. 641 pp. 17 plates.

This collection of strange stories and weird traditions has not been compiled with a view to creating *un frisson nouveau*, but to serve as a guide to the geography of Ghostland—a handbook to the Haunted Houses of Great Britain. Many historic tales of apparitions and supernaturally disturbed dwellings are imbedded in British literature; are frequently alluded to in journalistic and other publications, and are known to many by name, but by name only. Many people have heard of *The Demon of Tedworth*, *The Lord Lyttleton Ghost Story*, and other celebrated narratives of the uncanny kind, but it is rare to find anyone able to furnish particulars of them: to enable them to do this is the *raison d'etre* of this book.

Handbook to Hall Marks on Gold and Silver Plate of Great Britain and Ireland

By Wm. Chaffers

Revised by Cyril G. E. Bunt

In view of their importance, it is remarkable how few people, apart from members of ''the trade'' are familiar with the purport and intention of hall-marks on plate. This present handbook, now re-written and revised, gives instruction on the reading of hall marks.

Actually, the reading of marks on plate, once the fundamental principles are mastered, is as simple as reading a daily paper. Admittedly, one must be endowed with a more than ordinary memory to register mentally the numerous types of date letters indicating the various cycles; but such a feat need not be attempted when so complete a handbook as the present is available.

To the more experienced, the author offers a useful and reliable series of tables in which the marks of the several assay offices of Great Britain and Ireland are readily available. To the less advanced, there is an easy road to discovering the solution to the ''mystery'' of hall marks; and he does this in succinct and readable text free from that prolix, erudite phraseology in which writers on technical subjects often tend to indulge. Students will appreciate the instructive chronological table and the clarity of the drawings showing the various forms of the leopard's head, the lion and the marks used by provincial assay offices. And the different marks used in combination drawn from actual examples will be particularly welcome in assisting the beginner to understand and interpret the information the marks convey.

𝕬	1756–7	𝖆	1776–7	A	1796–7	𝖆	1816–7
𝕭	1757–8	𝖇	1777–8	B	1797–8	𝖇	1817–8
𝕮	1758–9	𝖈	1778–9	C	1798–9	𝖈	1818–9
𝕯	1759–60	𝖉	1779–80	D	1799–00	𝖉	1819–20
𝕰	1760–1	𝖊	1780–1	E	1800–1	𝖊	1820–1
𝕱	1761–2	𝖋	1781–2	F	1801–2	𝖋	1821–2
𝕲	1762–3	𝖌	1782–3	G	1802–3	𝖌	1822–3
𝕳	1763–4	𝖍	1783–4	H	1803–4	𝖍	1823–4
𝕴	1764–5	𝖎	1784–5	I	1804–5	𝖎	1824–5
𝕶	1765–6	𝖐	1785–6	K	1805–6	𝖐	1825–6
𝕷	1766–7	𝖑	1786–7	L	1806–7	𝖑	1826–7
𝕸	1767–8	𝖒	1787–8	M	1807–8	𝖒	1827–8
𝕹	1768–9	𝖓	1788–9	N	1808–9	𝖓	1828–9
𝕺	1769–70	𝖔	1789–90	O	1809–10	𝖔	1829–30
𝕻	1770–1	𝖕	1790–1	P	1810–1	𝖕	1830–1
𝕼	1771–2	𝖖	1791–2	Q	1811–2	𝖖	1831–2
𝕽	1772–3	𝖗	1792–3	R	1812–3	𝖗	1832–3
𝕾	1773–4	𝖘	1793–4	S	1813–4	𝖘	1833–4
𝕿	1774–5	𝖙	1794–5	T	1814–5	𝖙	1834–5
𝖀	1775–6	𝖚	1795–6	U	1815–6	𝖚	1835–6

Specimen Page

PRINTED IN GREAT BRITAIN BY
LOWE AND BRYDONE (PRINTERS) LIMITED, LONDON